TIME TO RUN

Adapted from the original
Allan Sloane screenplay

DIMENSION BOOKS
BETHANY FELLOWSHIP, INC.
Minneapolis, Minnesota

Copyright © 1973
BETHANY FELLOWSHIP, INC.

All rights reserved

ISBN 0-87123-538-2

A UNIMARK Production

Photos courtesy of Worldwide Pictures,
Frank Raymond

Song lyrics by Tedd Smith

DIMENSION BOOKS
are published by Bethany Fellowship, Inc.
6820 Auto Club Road
Minneapolis, Minnesota 55438

Printed in the United States of America

CONTENTS

CHAPTER 1	7
CHAPTER 2	11
CHAPTER 3	25
CHAPTER 4	37
CHAPTER 5	51
CHAPTER 6	71
CHAPTER 7	85
CHAPTER 8	97
CHAPTER 9	107
CHAPTER 10	123
CHAPTER 11	129

CHAPTER 1

Impatiently Jeff shifted from one foot to another as Michelle continued to read their poetry assignment aloud:

> "Still with unhurrying chase,
> And unperturbed pace,
> Came on the following Feet,
> And a Voice above their beat—
> 'Naught shelters thee who wilt not
>   shelter Me.'"

Now he pretended he was thoroughly bored. He leaned his head upon his shoulder, feigning sleep and began to snore.

"Come on." Michelle laughed, "We've got, um, three pages to go!"

"It takes this guy forever to say what's on his mind," protested Jeff. "He's really hung up on words."

It was a beautiful day to study in their special place—some secluded woods on a knoll. Michelle sat on a rock in the soft sunshine as the balmy breeze teased and coaxed loose wisps of hair from the confines of her pony tail.

"But it's... it's so beautiful... now listen," she cajoled.

> "But still within the little
>   children's eyes
>   Seems something, something that
>   replies,
>   They at least are for me, surely
>   for me."

"It sounds like you've already read it," Jeff declared.

"So?" Michelle challenged without looking up.

Jeff kneeled down beside her. "So give it to me in one sentence."

Michelle sighed, thought for a moment and then began to explain. "It's about how Francis Thompson tried to run away from God all his life. . . ."

"Um hmm . . ." Jeff pulled a long piece of grass from the ground and began to chew on it.

"But he couldn't," Michelle continued. "And that's why he called Him the 'Hound of Heaven.'" She looked down at her book and continued to read.

> "I fled Him down the nights and
>   down the days
>   I fled Him down the arches of
>   the years;

> I fled Him down the labyrinthine ways
> Of my own mind; and in the mist of tears . . ."

"Yeah," Jeff interrupted, "well, that's a pretty heavy subject. And I don't guess you can expect him to say it in a paragraph." He looked up at Michelle and grinned mischievously. "Hey, uh, you sure you didn't pick this assignment?"

Michelle laughed and aimed the book at Jeff, pretending to hit him. "Will you shut up and listen!" she demanded with mock frustration.

They bent their heads together over the book.

> "I hid from Him, and under running laughter
> Up vistaed hopes I sped . . ."

Jeff barely followed the words as Michelle continued to read. His eyes scanned the page, and suddenly he found a line that worked for him. "Hey! Uh . . .," he interrupted,

> "Let me greet you lip to lip.
> Let me twine you with caresses . . ."

His lips touched hers and he softly kissed her. Then he grabbed her shoulders and kissed her, fiercely and urgently.

CHAPTER 2

That afternoon the Civic Association met for their annual awards luncheon at the Carousel Inn. Waitresses balancing their large oval trays made precarious journeys to the tables as they picked their way over the TV camera cables on the floor.

The president of the association stepped to the podium. "We have one more item of business," he said, "and I'm sure this won't come as a surprise to anyone... that this year, our Industrial Achievement Award goes to... Warren Cole!" The men applauded and stood to their feet. Newsmen with sound equipment and cameras rushed forward to record the event for the early evening news.

Warren shook hands with the president and took the plaque which he presented to him. As the room full of people acknowledged his achievement and the members of the press gathered around, he flashed the plaque forward so that everyone could see it.

When the president sat down, Warren moved in toward the microphone. "Well, I, uh . . . ," he began to laugh. "I had an idea something like this might happen, so. . . ." And he took some notes for his acceptance speech out of his pocket and began to read them.

Television cameras also visited the Cragmont College campus that same afternoon. The reporter began his interview by taping some background remarks for the television audience. ". . . on campus this afternoon . . . and I've asked some of the students what they felt about FAEMAD. Well, let's find out . . . let's talk to some more of them."

Warren continued speaking to the association. "That complex that we've been building out there is not a — a pilot plant for power distribution. . . ."

The reporter addressed his first question to Jono, a student who was sitting casually on the campus union steps. "You've been listening—what about you?"

"Oh, man, that's not my bag. I'm not interested," Jono replied as he fluffed up his Afro for the cameraman.

"I think it's the greatest thing to hit this town since the electric toothpick," Jeff commented sarcastically as the reporter aimed his microphone at him. Some of the other kids began to snicker.

"Oh?" said the reporter. "That's a curious analogy. Uh, would you care to explain that?"

Jeff eyed him coldly. "Not really."

And at the Carousel Inn, Warren continued speaking. "We achieve more in satisfaction of our needs with fewer man hours of labor because of power and energy than any other country in the world."

The reporter knelt beside Michelle and Jeff. Jeff tried to ignore him by looking down at his books.

"Well now," persisted the reporter. "Wait, you obviously have a strong opinion."

Jeff shook his head. "Nah, uh uh." He looked at the reporter. "But I have lots of questions."

□

Fran continued to chop celery for the dinner salad. The early evening news was turned on in the den. "Does anyone happen to know what would go wrong if some little thing happened to our community atomic reactor?" Jeff's voice continued over the television.

Puzzled by that sound, Fran put down

her knife and rushed into the den.

". . . you know, and just how many jobs, uh, will automation take away from the people that just don't happen to have an engineering degree?" Jeff challenged. "And what are they going to do with the hot wastes? How much more of our shoreline will have to be cordoned off from public use whenever the demand is low and the heat generated gets rerouted back into the sea?"

Warren went on with his speech. "And we believe that this massive installation of ours is truly a living symbol of what man can accomplish when his heart and his mind are harnessed to the service of humanity."

Fran's mouth drew tight in a line of disapproval as Jeff continued to speak, "And isn't it true that FAEMAD's very biggest customer, uh, isn't going to be the little housewife with her washing machine. . . ."

The phone rang, and Fran walked toward it.

"It's going to be the Industrial-Military complex!" Jeff concluded.

Again the phone rang, and Fran grabbed the remote control from the table and turned off the TV so she could answer the phone. "Hello? . . . I know, Dottie, but . . . well, we've always given him freedom."

☐

Warren concluded his speech. "Thank you, gentlemen, very much for this gratifying award. Thank you." The Civic Association members stood and gave him a standing ovation.

Warren rushed home, and, as he entered the entrance hall, the phone was ringing again. Warren leafed through the mail on the credenza. When the phone rang again, he yelled at Fran. "I'll get it . . . Hello." As he listened, his face acquired a startled expression. He sighed resignedly. "Well, I'm afraid I can't make any comment about that until I've seen the transcript. . . . Well, you can quote me, 'no comment,' " he said impatiently. Warren began to hang up, but on impulse he decided to leave the phone off the hook.

"Warren," Fran defended as he walked into the kitchen, "I don't think he meant . . ."

"Looks like we're going to make the papers!" he interjected angrily.

☐

Jeff pulled the key from the ignition and parked his old brown van in the driveway. His truck was quite a contrast to Fran and

Warren's shiny new Chevys, and the three vehicles filled the driveway completely.

Jeff walked into the kitchen and put his books on the counter. "Hi." He walked over to his mother and gave her a peck on the cheek. "What's for dinner?" he continued as he took a carrot stick from the relish dish.

"Meatloaf... with rancor!" Fran warned.

Jeff paused for a moment and reached for a celery stalk.

"Your dad's in the den," Fran directed. Jeff turned to her with a tense glance. And then as if to reassure her, he kissed her again. "Oh, okay. No problem."

"Hi," said Jeff as he entered the den.

"Hey," Warren joked feebly, "where's your—your soapbox, eh?"

Jeff laughed his comment off. And as his eyes wandered over to the desk, he noticed the Civic Association award. "Oh! You had your little moment in the sun, and I had mine." Jeff picked up the plaque.

"Is that all you've got to say?" Warren demanded as he sat down.

"Congratulations," Jeff added a bit caustically.

"Looks like I've raised a kid with a whale of a big mouth."

" 'This above all, to thine own self be true,' " Jeff quoted.

Warren laughed. In spite of it all, he still wanted to keep the conversation friendly. "All right, you want to play Shakespeare?"

"Dinner's ready," Fran called as she tried to interrupt the impending argument.

"How about King Lear, act one, scene four, 'How sharper than a serpent's tooth is an ungrateful child,' " Warren countered.

Jeff grimaced, and in annoyance walked toward the dining room.

"Will you two stop it! Sit down!" Fran pleaded.

"Jeff, look, I wouldn't have minded so much if you had made your case on facts. I mean, really, if it bugged you that much, you should have talked to me." Warren sat down at the table.

Jeff took off his jacket, but he remained standing. "Okay, how about twenty minutes next Thursday, between microcircuits?"

Warren chose not to reply to that comment.

"Anyway," Jeff continued, "you have a way of bending everything to your radioactive logic. Maybe I'm more interested in truth," Jeff said deliberately.

"Truth!" challenged Warren as he jumped to his feet.

17

Jeff left the dining room and rushed up the stairs.

"Warren," said Fran, "please, can't it wait until after dinner?"

"Apparently it can't." He rushed away from the table after Jeff.

In her frustration, Fran stabbed the meatloaf she had been slicing. The meatloaf would have to be leftovers. She buried her head in her hands.

Warren started up the stairs. "Jeff!"

Jeff angrily slammed his door shut.

"Jeff!"

Jeff threw his jacket on his bed and jammed his ear phones on his head. He turned on his tape player and tried to immerse himself in the rock music it played.

Warren thrust Jeff's door open.

"Hey, you're supposed to knock before coming in here!"

Warren walked over to the tape recorder and snapped it off. "I'm not going to knock in my own house," he replied softly.

Jeff pulled off his earphones and drew himself up in a "Heil Hitler" salute. "Yessir!"

Warren swallowed. "Ah, what are y' . . . come on, Jeff, you don't have to do that. I'm your father."

"Next reason." Jeff thought for a moment and decided to face the issue at hand. "Look, I was just one of a hundred faces down there."

Warren whirled around. "Come on, you actually think they picked you out of the crowd because of your good looks?" "Don't be stupid! You were a set-up!" he shouted. "They knew who you were, and they knew who your father was, too." He lowered his voice. "No, you've been had, pal, you just fell into it . . . that's all."

"Look," replied Jeff, "aren't you being a little bit paranoid?"

"I'm simply trying to explain to you, rationally, the consequences."

"Look, I said what I mean, and I meant what I said. Don't I have that right?" Jeff countered.

"No. You don't!"

"Apparently I don't!" Angrily Jeff turned toward his closet and reached inside.

"No, you don't have that right, not to condemn my work, no."

Jeff backed out of his closet with a duffle bag. He threw the bag onto his bed and went to his dresser and began pulling out his clothes.

"FAEMAD put this house over your head, you . . ." Warren shouted.

Jeff continued to rush around his room,

pulling out clothes and throwing them on his bed.

"I mean, just what . . . everything you . . . just where do you think it all came from?"

Blindly Jeff stuffed the clothes into his bag. "Money, money, money," he muttered.

"Sure, money. All right, what's wrong with that, huh? Just what have you contributed to the family?"

Jeff turned around and faced his father. "I'm getting out of your house!"

He pulled the drawstring tight on his bag and walked into the bathroom.

"I'm finding that heavy father trip you are constantly running is really the ultimate bummer of the world!"

In frustration, Warren ran his fingers through his hair. "Would you mind translating that for me, please?"

Jeff grabbed some toiletries out of the medicine cabinet. "What we're really talking about, isn't it, is your image? And how I have to live up to it." He slammed the door shut and crammed the articles into the top of his bag.

"Maybe I'm concerned with how you think," Warren replied.

"How about what I think?" Jeff stood

back and looked at his father. "Well, I think that image is tarnished, *Daddy*, and I really don't think I can live with that!" He reached over the head of his bed and pulled a large poster photo of Michelle from the wall.

"Come on, Jeff, will you use your head?" Warren pleaded.

Jeff grabbed up his belongings and left the room shouting, "Look, it's my head!"

He ran down the stairs. "I don't know what I am, but I'm not one of your machines." He turned his head around and looked at his father. "You can't program *me* to your specifications. I'm me! And that's all I want to be."

He rushed toward the entrance hall with Warren close behind. As the commotion got closer Fran entered the hallway.

"Jeff, wait a minute!" Warren called. For an instant Jeff stopped, expecting his father would ask him to stay. "How about my credit card?" demanded Warren as he held out his hand.

Jeff slammed his bag down and yanked his wallet out of his pocket.

"Are you both out of your minds?" Fran said. It was too incredulous for her to believe.

Jeff slapped the credit card into Warren's hand. "All yours!" He dashed out of the house, slamming the door as he departed.

Angrily Warren clamped his jaws tight so he would not say anything further. In the silence, Fran turned to Warren with accusing eyes, "Are you satisfied?" she said bitterly.

CHAPTER 3

Angrily Jeff drove his van through the city streets. He took an eight-track cartridge off the dashboard and shoved it into the cassette player. He adjusted the volume and turned it up louder, attempting to drown out the echoes of the fight with his father. It was a recording of Michelle's song.

"And he looks a million miles ahead
And two thousand years behind
And he travels on,
That will be his song,
'Cause he is the traveling kind.
And at night the sky will blanket him
And the earth will be his pillow
The sun will welcome him each day,
As he rests 'neath weeping willow
And the things he owns are on his back,
And his work shows in his hands.
And his friends are miles and miles
   ahead
In a far, far distant land.

And he traveled on another road,
The longest of them all
Where he proved what love was all about
By suffering for man's fall.
And he showed in doing what he meant
When he laid down his life for a friend
The greatest thing a man could give,
The hardest road to travel.
If you look to see his hands and brow
You will know he understands.
'Cause he's been on the road you're
   traveling now,
He is that kind of traveling man."

As the song continued, Jeff traveled down the traffic-clogged city street, trying to decide what to do and where to go. He reached down to change gears. Silently he drove on, clenching his jaws.

□

Warren sat on the plaid sofa in the den trying to concentrate on FAEMAD's control sheet. As Fran paced the floor, Warren attempted to explain his argument with Jeff. "I was just trying to figure out when we had our first run-in, the one that started the whole avalanche." He gazed intently at Fran. "You see him so much more than I do, honey, does he talk to you?"

"He used to."

"Yeah. I was just trying to go back to that first mistake," Warren said in puzzlement.

"I know what mine was.... I tried to explain my husband to my son," Fran said softly.

Warren didn't understand. "Was there really that much to explain?"

There was an awkward moment of silence for Fran could not think of any more words of explanation. Miserably Warren turned away. "I'll make some coffee," Fran said to cover the uncomfortable moment.

☐

As the sunlight entered the van in a thin frame around the curtains, Jeff awoke with a start. He looked outside and saw the campus parking lot was filling up as other students made their way to class. Hastily he unzipped his sleeping bag and tried to do double-time getting ready for his first-hour class.

Dave Green, Warren Cole's assistant at FAEMAD, was invited to be guest lecturer for the cybernetics class. As he attempted to explain his illustration to the class, Dave drew computer symbols on the chalkboard. "And that's how we come to information retrieval," he concluded.

"Are you saying that in cybernetics the machine substitutes for the human brain?" inquired a student.

Dave attempted to illustrate it another way. "When you pick up a telephone and dial, that substitutes for what we used to call the 'hello girl,' the operator. But in computers, the information retrieval supplements the human brain."

Michelle was hardly aware of what Dave Green was saying. Worried because Jeff hadn't shown up for class, she glanced over her shoulder out the window and turned around occasionally to peer out the open doorway.

Dave continued lecturing, "You're doing what the human brain does, and you're doing it faster and more accurately, and it remembers better! Man improving on his own creation," Dave theorized.

Jono got Dave's attention and raised a question. "Can the computer think?"

"In the present state of cybernetic knowledge, a computer can only do what it is told to do."

"Doesn't decision-making require thinking?" inquired another student.

"Computers are able to make decisions," Dave replied, "but only based on the information given to the computer by the computer programmer."

At this point the professor stood up to bring the session to an end. "I wish we had longer, Mr. Green, but we have five minutes to get to the next class."

As the class began to disperse, some interested students gathered around Dave. He picked up his attaché case and smiled. "Look, if you all really want to see how this plugs in, why don't we set up a ten-dollar tour of the installation?"

"Do we get credit?" joked a student. Dave grinned good-naturedly in reply and walked out of the classroom with the professor.

Two of the last people to leave were Michelle and Mark. Jeff hadn't shown up yet, and she was beginning to worry.

"Hey, look," Mark said encouragingly, "don't worry about it; he's, he's around."

Michelle responded with a thankful grin. "Okay. See ya'." But she still wondered what had happened to Jeff.

Jeff tore across the parking lot and on to the campus lawn. He ran up the steps of Moreland Hall. Deep in thought, he ran down some stairs and suddenly spun around as Dave grabbed his arm. "Hey, Jeff," Dave said in a surprised voice.

Being caught off-guard, Jeff tried to greet him. "Uh . . . ," he began.

"Missed you this morning," said Dave as he dropped Jeff's arm.

"Yeah, I blew it!" Jeff said lightly. Then a little more seriously, he replied, "Sorry, Dave. Did I miss, uh, much?"

"Fifty minutes summary of everything I know!" Dave joked.

Jeff laughed uncomfortably.

Dave asked in a serious tone, "Seen the morning paper?"

"No, uh, what's in it?"

"You are!" Dave replied matter-of-factly.

Jeff groaned and turned away.

"Got a minute?" asked Dave.

Jeff was in no mood for a heart-to-heart talk, and quickly he made an excuse. "Hey, not right now, I'm due at English 102," he fumbled helplessly.

"Okay. I'll see you tonight."

Jeff did not know what to say. "Whatever," he replied as he shrugged his shoulders and stalked away.

He walked over to a nearby newstand, put a dime in it and pulled out the morning paper. There he was—right on the front page! In a large headline centered over his photo and three columns were the words,

"SON BLASTS FATHER'S ACHIEVEMENT."

Michelle spotted him. She ran up the steps and waited for him to look up from his paper. "Should I ask for your autograph?" she inquired with a teasing smile.

He rolled up the paper and snapped her affectionately on the nose.

☐

That afternoon Jeff and Michelle returned to their place on the knoll and tried to study. But Jeff's cassette player and the scenery which encircled them rivaled their attention. The day was better designed for romping in the woods than it was for studying.

"Whenever we're together
Things start turning bright
Because we understand each other.
The sunshine that surrounds you
Turns the dark to light
Because we understand each other.
Look into my eyes, see my smile,
  feel my touch.
You understand you have it all.

Travel through my mind and
Leave the imprint of the warm
I'm feeling now . . . forever. . . .

So many times I've tried to
Play at what I am
Wanting to be strong,
Wanting to belong,

And then you touch my mind
With everything you are,
Suddenly it's spring,
Winter's chill is gone. . . .
And as you weave a spell,
You're handing me a key,
Suddenly I'm free . . .
Because we understand each other. . . .

I know at times I've got to
Wear you down, but somehow
Knowing that I've got you around,
Makes me feel the sunshine that
Has got to follow rain . . .
Because we understand each other."

A sunshiny day requires playing hide-and-seek in the woods. When they came to the footbridge, Michelle jumped up on the railing and walked across it tight-rope fashion. And Jeff found a good climbing tree and did his special Tarzan routine.

☐

English Lit. 106 met for a seminar. As the students discussed the poem they were studying, Jeff was more involved in printing on a 3" x 5" card.

Jono entered the discussion. "Okay, hey, listen, uh, it's nice poetry—days, years, ways, tears. But rhyme doesn't get it for me."

"But what about the meaning?" asked the professor.

"Uh, well," began Mark, "something's chasing him, uh, the something, something uh, of his mind, uh—paranoia!"

A chorus of agreement went up from several of the students.

"The 'Hound of Heaven' is God," interjected Michelle.

"Now she'll begin preaching," thought Jeff. "Look, a poem should, uh, be—not mean," he suggested hastily.

"But you have to bring something to a poem; if all you're doing is looking at the words . . . ," continued Michelle.

"Hey! Hold on a sec," exclaimed Jeff. "I hear you saying I can't appreciate this thing because I'm not into God. Well, I'm not a murderer, and I read 'Crime and Punishment.' "

The point had been made, and Michelle laughed graciously.

The professor stood up. "All right, I

33

think it's fair that we each interpret poetry from our frame of reference." He looked over at Michelle. "Michelle, you believe the 'Hound of Heaven' is God. Can you support that from the work itself?"

Michelle looked down at the book she was holding and began to read. "Alas, thou knowest not how little worthy of any love thou art."

Now Jeff was feeling defensive, embarrassed that his girl friend should be so hung up on her belief.

Michelle continued.

"Whom wilt thou find to love
   ignoble thee,

 Save me, save only me."

She looked up at the professor. "We're unworthy of God's love, and yet he loves us."

"You lose me on the 'thees' and 'thous,' " Jono rejoined.

Michelle laughed good-naturedly.

"Who'll finish it for us?" asked the professor as he looked around the classroom. His eyes locked on Jeff. "Jeff?"

Jeff looked up. "I didn't get that far."

The professor's face registered disapproval, and he looked around the class again. As his eyes wandered back to Michelle, he smiled paternally at her. She was the most interested in the poem. "Michelle, will you end it for us, please."

She looked down at her book.

"Ah, fondest, blindest, weakest,
I am He whom thou seekest,
thou dravest love from thee who draves
    me."

"You got a date!" cracked Jeff, and Michelle laughed.

One of the students looked at the clock. "It's time to go."

The other students murmured their agreement and began to gather up their books. "All right," said the professor as he dismissed them formally.

"Hey, Jono, where you going?" called Jeff as he stopped him outside the classroom.

"I got to shoot over to the library."

"Hey, do me a favor, uh, will you?"

"Sure," replied Jono.

Jeff handed a file card to him. "Post that on the board, will you?"

"Yeah. Hey," he said as he began reading it, "guitars, amps, skis . . ."

"Yeah, well, I need the bread," explained Jeff.

"Okay, see you later."

CHAPTER 4

Warren entered the dining room with mugs of coffee for Dave and him. They continued the discussion which had begun at the dinner table.

"You brought him up to be a self-reliant, independent human being," said Dave.

Warren sat down.

". . . and the moment he cuts loose a little . . . ," Dave reasoned. "So he shot his mouth off . . ."

"It has nothing to do with that," Warren replied in a frustrated voice. "Nor the fact that he was arrested two times for speeding."

"Three times," corrected Dave.

Ignoring Dave's comment, Warren continued, ". . . or totaling the Olds." He sighed and settled back on the sofa. "Or even making a fool out of himself on the tube."

"So what is eating you?" quizzed Dave.

During the conversation Fran had entered the room, and she sat quietly. Apprehensively, she looked at Warren as he talked.

"How do you get through to someone who opposes everything you stand for, and possibly you?"

Fran abruptly set down her coffee cup and jumped up from her chair, unable to listen any longer. "Warren . . ." she pleaded in a broken voice.

"Is that bending the truth?"

Fran didn't reply as she rushed from the room.

□

Jeff and Michelle walked across the campus to the parking lot. "Hey, you're the one that's always selling faith. How about some in me?" suggested Jeff.

Their eyes met for a moment, and Michelle looked down as she began to explain. "You know how uptight my landlady gets."

"Yeah . . . Maybe she likes pizza?"

Michelle began to laugh quietly. Jeff stopped suddenly and turned to her.

"Hey, uh, what's the matter? You really don't want me to come home with you!"

"Trouble is, I do," Michelle responded

softly as she played with a buttonhole on his jacket.

While Jeff showered, Michelle used this opportunity to mend his shirt. As he entered the room, she put his shirt down and pulled another from the duffel bag. She began to inspect it for any loose buttons.

"Ah, yes," joked Jeff, "here we have Mrs. Ungerdunger, our typical, but beautiful American housewife—and mother!, who doesn't know she's on 'Candid Commercial-l-l'! And now, for an honest opinion of our product..." He held out his hand as if it were a microphone and aimed it at Michelle.

"Why," she drawled, "little ol' me on 'Candid Commercial'? Where's the camera?"

"Right here, little lady," Jeff replied as he walked over by the TV set.

Michelle straightened up and preened for the TV and began to give her "candid" opinion. "I just washed these clothes in Grubby's new improved super-strength detergent." She pretended to inspect the shirt. "Why, these aren't too clean!"

The "announcer" quickly tried to cover up his "candid" interview. "Ah, yes, well, uh, thank you, Mrs. Ungerdunger!"

Michelle knelt beside the duffel bag and

began to drag out more clothes. "As a matter of fact, they were much cleaner before I washed them!"

"Ah, yes, uh, thank you, Mrs. Ungerdunger!"

Michelle interrupted. "Ah do believe this is the dirtiest set of laundry ah've ever seen!"

"Mrs. Ungerdunger!" the "announcer" cautioned and pleaded.

Michelle grabbed all the clothes and crammed them into Jeff's face, her Southern accent rising to a near screech, "Looks like someone slept in a truck all night long!"

They dissolved in giggles as Jeff came up on his knees close to Michelle. He kissed her tenderly and gazed at her. "Yeah, we could really make it here, just the two of us."

Michelle's expression became serious and she touched his face almost apologetically before she stood up. She did not know how to explain her new way of life to him, and for a moment, she silently stood with her back to him.

Jeff gathered up his clothes and began tossing them into his duffel bag.

"I almost forgot the history notes..." Michelle began.

Jeff frowned and continued jamming the

clothes into his bag. "Yeah, that's cool," he responded dejectedly as he began to pull on his boots.

Michelle turned, but she continued to look down. "We've got that seminar thing in the morning at your dad's place.... Will you pick me up?"

Jeff got up and picked up his bag. "Don't count on it."

"What's that supposed to mean?" Michelle inquired as Jeff walked out into the hallway. He snatched open the outside door and stalked outside, leaving the door open behind him.

Michelle stood numbly in the doorway and struggled with the thoughts of her boyfriend's needs as they clashed with her recently-found faith.

□

The siren wound down as the police car with its red light flashing stopped behind Warren's car. He waited for Officer Angelo Soldini as he came to the car window.

"Hey, Warren, what do you think you're doing?"

Already Warren had his license out of his billfold and with a tight jaw he replied exasperatedly, "Just give me a ticket, will you, Angie?"

"Yeah, but this is a built-up zone. Now

you had to be doing at least sixty. . . ."

"Skip the lecture, please," Warren interrupted.

"Okay," Angie sighed, "let's have it." Warren placed his license in Angie's outstretched palm. As Angie began writing out the ticket, Warren picked up his car phone.

"Sharon, I'm going to be about five minutes late this morning." He hung up the phone.

"Well, we will sure miss you at the golf course," Angie said, as he tried to brighten up the conversation.

Warren didn't respond.

"Boy, you could hit that ball a ton," Angie continued as he handed Warren the ticket.

Suddenly Warren decided that he would attempt something.

"Listen, Angie, I wonder if you could do me a favor; I, uh . . ."

Angie moved his hand in a "name it" gesture.

"Jeff and I had a kind of a, a problem last night, and he's left the house. I wondered if you could kind of, um, keep an eye out for him; you know, um, nothing official." He signed the ticket and handed it to Angie.

"Listen, I got three of my own. . . . How do you think I got the gray hair?"

☐

Jeff pulled his van through the guard gate at FAEMAD's entrance. As he stopped, the guard came to the window. "Morning, Jeff," he called as he checked his watch.

"Morning. I'm here for Dave Green's class," he explained.

The guard handed him an I.D. badge. "They're on their way down to the Master Control."

"Okay." Jeff glanced at the I.D. badge and tossed it onto the dashboard.

The guard leaned back toward the window. "Hey, don't forget, you're supposed to wear that."

With a bored gesture, Jeff waved him away and drove on in. He passed the fountain and made a sharp turn into the Visitor Parking section. It was already filled with other students' cars. He pinned the I.D. on his coat and got out of the car and entered the building.

In the corridor outside Master Control, Dave Green continued his lecture tour. "Come on in," he invited the students as they entered the corridor. "Everybody fill in around the window here."

On the other side of the window was FAEMAD's gigantic Master Control complete with computer panels, gauges, print-out boards and numerous colored blinking lights. Here Warren Cole and a technician were already at work checking data which was spewing out of a print-out board.

"All right now," Dave continued, "you realize that everything you have seen is run from right here in Master Control. That includes the reactor, desalinization, intake, fresh water output, uh, temperature maintenance, steam conversion, turbine speed, power start and stop."

As he went on with his lecture, he crossed to the entry marked "Security Systems" and opened the door by slotting his special I.D. card into a groove above the doorknob.

By now Warren recognized this was Jeff's cybernetics class. He left Master Control and entered Security Systems where a security guard was monitoring Master Control and the surrounding corridors with closed circuit cameras. "Let me sit in there a minute, Curt, huh?" he said to the guard.

"Sure." The guard gathered up his papers and moved to an adjacent chair as Warren took his place behind the camera controls.

Again Dave pulled out his I.D. card; this time to open the door into Master Control.

"Security's pretty tight, huh?" observed a student.

"Well," said Dave as he waved the hesitating students inside, "security can electronically seal off this entire plant."

Warren stared intently at the monitor as it picked up a picture of the students entering Master Control. A loudspeaker in Security Systems carried Dave's voice into the room.

"Then we need one of these authorized key cards to release the locking mechanism. We use them at all times here in Master Control," Dave explained. The students fanned out and began inspecting the equipment in Master Control. "Come on in, everybody, but please, whatever you do, don't touch anything, all right?" He threaded his way through the group of students to a clearing beside the computer board.

"Now. Our research and development program has put us ahead of most other countries in the programming and control of atomic energy."

As he noticed Jeff entering Master Control, Warren moved in closer to the monitor.

"And actually the biggest loads in the history of atomic reactive power are stored right here...," Dave went on, "programmed for all conceivable combinations of demand and circumstance."

Jeff joined the group of students, but even here he felt uncomfortable; it seemed his father's presence permeated the entire building.

The monitoring camera, with its red light glaring, moved from its neutral position till its unblinking eye stared directly at Jeff. As it zeroed in on him, he began to shift uncomfortably.

Dave proceeded with his lecture. "It all boils down to one reel of tape controlling the whole thing and," he joked, "filling out the city payroll at the same time."

Warren looked at the monitor as the camera was fixed on Jeff. It was not his nature to spy on his son, but today feelings overcame reticence.

A girl standing next to Michelle nudged her and whispered as she recognized Jeff. Startled, Michelle turned around and looked at him. They exchanged smiles and then turned their attention back to Dave.

"... automatically cutting substations in; cutting others out. The data that has been designed into these machines..."

Jeff looked up and, still bothered by the camera's unflinching stare, began to slowly drift in behind the other students.

". . . enable us to control power plants, automatically cutting in appropriate substations and cutting out others, feeding power where it's needed."

As the camera followed Jeff around the room, he ducked behind the heads of the other students, then suddenly reappeared on the monitor with his fist forming a circle over his eye like a telescope— a silent "I spy" to his father!

Embarrassed, Warren glanced at the security guard to see if he noticed. Abruptly Warren stood up. "I'm sorry, pal," he said as he left the cubicle.

The wandering red light on the camera went off, and the camera was returned to its neutral position.

"Now," Dave went on, "the number of man hours that have been invested in this project are comparable to all the time devoted to our space program."

Jeff left the group of students and went out the door.

"So what happens if somebody pushes the wrong button?" inquired Chris, one of the students.

47

"It screws up the tape," another student suggested.

"Doom, doom, doom," replied Chris in a sotto melancholy voice.

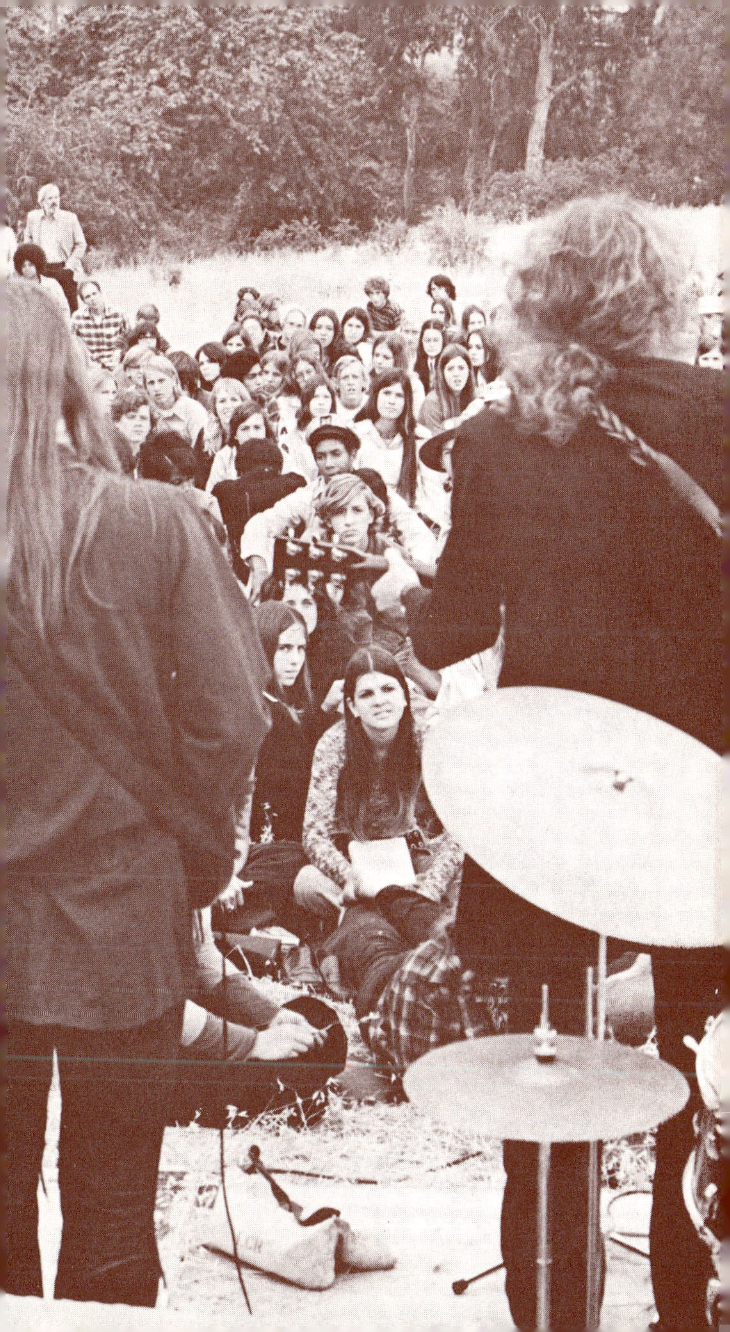

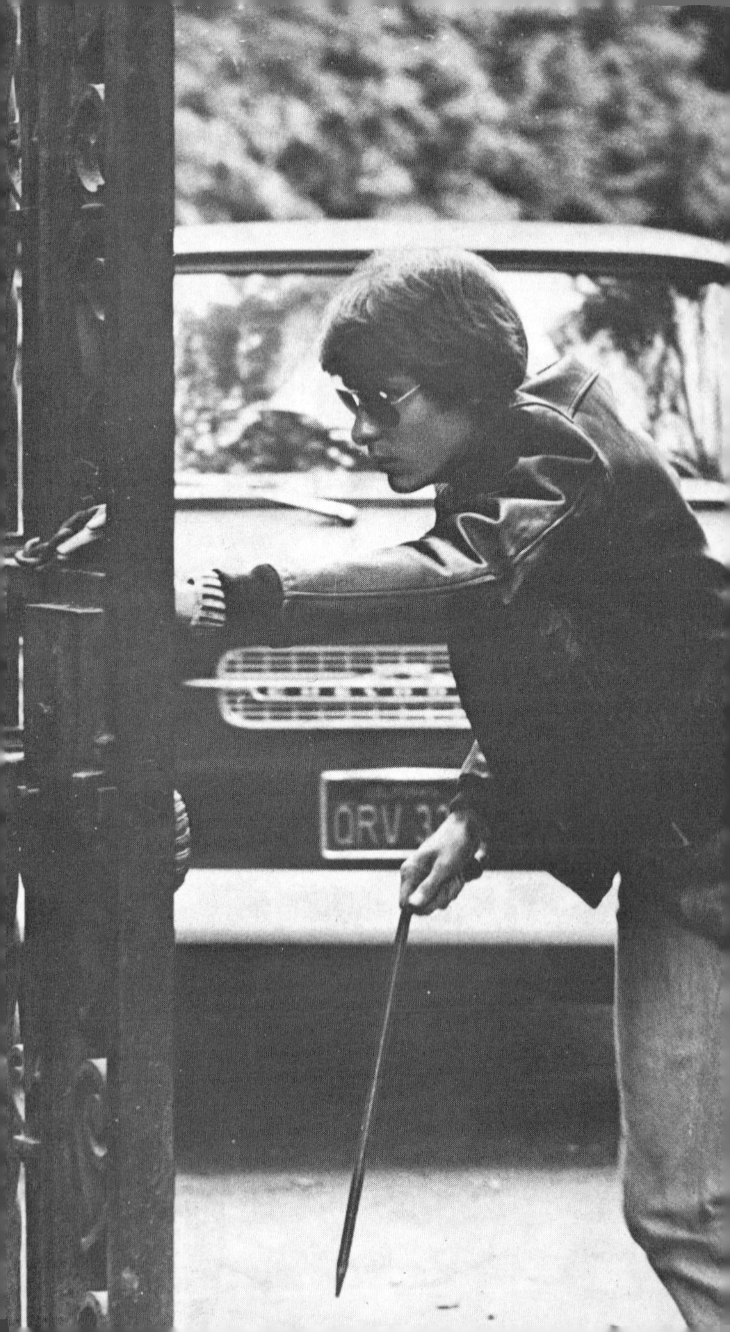
QRV 3

CHAPTER 5

The only way Jeff was going to open the heavy old iron gates was to break the big rusted chain which held it shut. He rummaged around in his van until he found a crowbar. He pried the chain off the gate and pushed it open. With a heavy clang, the gate seemed to shudder as it was opened.

Jeff ran back to his van and drove through, ignoring the large red and white sign which proclaimed, "NO TRESPASSING—Violators Will be Prosecuted." He jumped out of his van and pulled the gate closed, securing the chain behind him.

The van followed the narrow road which led past a boarded-up old shed. Jeff drove on between some trees and some overgrown remains of a flower garden. In the distance was a huge mansion, Spanish-style, pink stucco with a red roof. Jeff proceeded on to the mansion and parked his van under a carport.

This was a good hiding place. He could

hole up here and think for awhile while he decided what to do. The only sound here was the chirping of some birds.

☐

Fran felt like an intruder, a small ant in a busy ant colony. Feeling uncomfortably out of place, she wandered around campus and lingered here and there, hoping to find some clue about Jeff's whereabouts.

Leaning against the ad building was Jeff's friend, Jono. Fran rushed over to him.

"Jono..."

"Oh, hi, Mrs. Cole. How are you?"

"Just fine. Have you seen Jeff?"

"Uh, no, not for a couple of days. No." With nothing more to say, he walked away. Fran stood there awkwardly, wondering what she should do next. She spotted Michelle standing nearby with three girlfriends, and she hurried over to her.

"Michelle..."

Michelle looked up and stopped her talking.

Fran continued. "Could I see you for a moment, please?"

Michelle nodded, and the other girls murmured their goodbyes and left. Fran and Michelle eyed each other for a moment.

Both were a bit hesitant; Fran was aware she was breaking one of Jeff's moral codes by talking to his girlfriend about him, and Michelle felt uncomfortable being approached by Jeff's mother. After some small talk, they walked off to Michelle's apartment.

Fran sat on the window ledge while Michelle busied herself arranging cookies and cups on a tray while the teapot began to boil.

"I'm open to just about anything," Fran said, "I mean, you're so much closer to him than we are.... For a time there I thought you were going to get engaged.... If that isn't too old-fashioned," she added.

Michelle gave Fran a noncommittal smile, but she did not answer.

"Then when you stopped seeing each other so much, Jeff said the competition was too tough...."

Fran waited, her silence demanding some kind of explanation of Jeff's comment. For a moment Michelle was thoughtful. Then, without turning away from her preparations of refreshments, she began to explain.

"I guess he meant Jesus...." She slowly turned around and sat down. "You know it's really strange, because I have so much more love to give him now. And he's miles away . . . and he can't see it."

Thoughtfully Fran listened, a troubled and quizzical expression on her face. She was more interested in another aspect of their relationship. "Does he talk to you about us—about his family?"

"Sometimes," Michelle replied honestly.

Fran got up and wandered around the room and attempted to think. She looked around Michelle's room. On one wall was a collage of pictures of Jeff and Michelle. In several photos Jeff was playing his guitar. In a couple he was in a group of kids, and some were wearing "One Way" T-shirts. Next to the pictures Michelle had tacked up a large poster which contained a silhouette and the words, "WANTED . . . Jesus Christ." As Fran stared at the pictures, Michelle walked over and joined her.

"Jeff took most of those. . . ."

"Is he interested in . . . religion?"

"Oh, that was a concert," replied Michelle. "He plays sometimes. Sunday afternoons we usually have a thing going at the park. . . ."

☐

Early that Sunday the crowd gathered at the park. As stragglers made their way up the hill, the sounds of earlycomers' singing greeted them.

"We can be together for now and forever
I love you, I love you, I love you
I love you, I love you, I love you
And when I'm praying, I hear Him
  saying
I love you, oh, I love you, I love you.
People all over the world
They're opening up
They're coming around,
They're saying . . .
I love you, I love you, I love you
I love you, I love you, I love you."

Several vans and cars were parked in the lot at the bottom of the hill, and kids hurried up the path to join the group. Dave Green parked his convertible, and he and Fran approached some kids who were starting up the hill.

" 'Scuse me," said Dave, "can you tell me where it's happening?"

With a friendly smile, Rick replied, "Yeah, it's up on the hill."

As he turned to leave, Dave mumbled

a "thank you" and took Fran's arm.

Rick thrust a pamphlet toward Dave. "Here, take a couple of these with you; it's a long walk; they'll keep you busy."

Dave took the pamphlet and glanced at it, and then he tried to hand it back. Amused, Fran walked on ahead. "Oh, it's not our thing, really, thank you, 'scuse me," Dave said in an embarrassed voice as he turned again to leave.

"Well, it's not exactly a 'thing,' you know," suggested Rick. "It could be your whole life!"

Dave stopped, annoyed. Fran was getting impatient. "Look, that works for you, fine, but I just don't go along with it. 'Scuse me," he said as he took Fran's arm and tried to duck around Rick, but Rick followed right behind.

"Would you mind telling me what you do believe in?" Rick asked.

Dave turned around and gave Rick a hard look. Exasperated, he glanced at Fran and sighed. Then he turned to Rick and firmly said, "In my book, I just don't believe in miracles. I believe in what works."

"Would you believe in how Christ worked for me?" Rick said sincerely. "See, I had three felony raps for possession.

I was in and out of every kind of do-it-yourself thing to kick the habit. At one point, I was so far down, I felt like dying."

Fran became interested and shifted forward to get a better look at Rick. Dave raised an eyebrow and looked at Fran to see her reaction to Rick's comments.

"And then somebody touched me and told me I could change my whole life right around if I'd just let Jesus help me." As the words tumbled out, Rick grinned a big, happy, sincere smile. "Jesus is real, brother, praise God!" He pointed upward.

Eager to get away from this intense young man, Dave said firmly, "Thank you." Under his breath he muttered to Fran, "This must be the place."

As the singing subsided at the top of the hill, Randy, a young man with long, curly hair and a moustache stood up and began to talk. He folded his arms over his Bible as he began telling the story of the "Good Samaritan" to the young people.

"We're singing about love. But what is this love, this love we sing about? Love is a pretty general term today. It could mean anything from something someone might say to someone when they wanted to go to bed with them to an ecstatic spiritual feeling of fulfillment, deep inside."

Fran and Dave arrived at the top of the hill, and they began to study the group of young people.

"I don't think he's here, Fran," said Dave as Randy continued to speak.

"But real love as taught by the Bible is giving. The Bible says in Luke 10 when a 'legal expert' asked Jesus about God's command to love thy neighbor that Jesus replied with this story."

As Randy spoke, several young people followed along, their heads bent over their Bibles.

"It seems there was this man traveling from Jericho to Jerusalem; that could have been from Los Angeles to San Francisco, for that matter, and he fell among some thieves and they beat him up, took his money, took his clothes, and pushed him off to the side of the road and just generally ripped him off."

Michelle was among those listening to Randy, but occasionally her attention wandered, and she looked around for Jeff. When she spotted Fran and Dave standing in the group behind her, she waved a pleased greeting.

"This priest came along," continued

Randy. "He was a very holy individual. He looked at the man lying at the side of the road and decided that he didn't want to get involved, so he passed him by.

"Then an assistant or somebody from the temple came along and he looked at the guy lying there and rushed right by, because he didn't have the time to be involved." Randy paused. "That seems to me where most of us are. That seems to be the human condition. We—we need this help, and we reach out for this help, but nobody hears us, because everybody's just too busy."

As these words reached her, Fran listened more intently.

"But that's not the end of the story. Another man came down the road. He was what the Bible called a 'despised Samaritan.' We would probably call him the last man on the face of the earth to help anybody, because nobody ever helped him.

"The Samaritans had their own little ghetto, you know. He knew all about pain, so he walked over to the man at the side of the road, and he bandaged him up and took care of him.

"Maybe you've been waylaid by the side of life's highway or maybe you know someone who has."

Fran's head was bowed, and a frown creased her forehead as Randy's words reached a tender spot.

"Jesus loves you, you know. He wants to help you. And He proved His love for you by dying on the cross for you. Open up and accept that love He has to offer."

As he completed his talk, the kids began to sing another song.

"Jesus came into the world
To set us all free,
To show us the way
Love us, He laid down His life,
Loving us, forgiving us, always . . .
Oh, Lord, we need you so, need you."

Feeling a bit awkward, Fran and Dave stood near the group and listened to them. Michelle was beaming and she walked up to Fran and hugged her. Fran stood stiffly, and she looked at Dave who was looking somewhat bemused.

□

As Dave drove off, Fran walked across the yard and let herself in at the front door. She walked across the dining room and through the sliding glass doors where she saw Warren lounging on the patio.

"Hi!" Fran called out.

"Where have you been all afternoon? I've been home since two o'clock."

"Well," Fran explained, "I went to a meeting with Dave . . . some of Michelle's friends were having."

Not understanding, Warren frowned.

"I thought Jeff might be there, but he wasn't."

Warren sat there, still frowning.

"Then we just sat and talked and . . . the time just got away."

"Four hours?" Warren declared in an incredulous voice.

"Well," Fran replied defensively, "it's not exactly normal for you to be home on Sunday afternoons. Maybe you'd better start mimeographing your schedule," she concluded angrily as she whirled around and rushed into the house.

Warren got up and followed her inside. "How often do you have these little chats?" he asked sarcastically.

"Dave's a good listener!"

☐

Early the next morning Warren got right to the point with Dave. Angrily he warned him, "The next time she wants to cry on your shoulder, why don't you try taking her to lunch?"

"Now wait a minute..." Dave said as he turned and faced Warren. "She asked me to take her there. And, probably because you'd have taken out your slide rule and proven there wasn't any God!"

"God? Oh, come on, Dave, will you; it's just a fad. What was it, rock last year, peace last week, pot yesterday and Jesus today, and who knows what tomorrow," he replied laughing.

"Yes," said Dave thoughtfully, "but what if there is something more? What if those kids really do have something?"

When Warren ignored him, Dave entered Master Control and, with a parting shot, remarked, "I'm a scientist; I'm open."

"Open?" Warren exclaimed. He jumped up and followed Dave. "Open?" He walked over to where Dave was standing at a computer panel. "Do you think all this was prayed into existence? It took intelligence and hard work, yours and mine, and alot of other people before us."

"Which only proves what God could have done if He had a Federal grant!" Dave retorted sarcastically.

Warren returned to the Conference Room. "Oh, that's funny, that's really funny."

☐

Michelle rode her bike to the steps of her apartment building. She gathered up her books and walked up the stairs to the entranceway where she checked her mailbox. As she approached her apartment door, she noticed a note with her name on it taped to the door. Puzzled, she opened up the note, and out fell a small white daisy with a map and a poem which read: "Iron Gates Will Make You Wait, But Don't Be Late, Don't Hesitate."

Michelle disposed of her books in her apartment and returned with the map to her bike. The map led her to the iron gates with the rusty chain. A cluster of daisies was stuck through the chain. She pulled the flowers away, wondering how she would get in.

After a few hesitant tugs, the chain broke away, and she rode her bike in.

Inside from an overgrown flower bed, Jeff peeped out at Michelle, moving cautiously lest she see him.

Michelle headed down the driveway, looking right and left and ahead in search of Jeff.

He kept out of sight and moved cautiously alongside her through the grass. Then he rushed to get ahead of her, running as fast as he could and leaping over long weeds and fallen branches.

Suddenly Michelle stopped her bike and looked up as she heard an ape-like sound coming from overhead.

"Ooh-a-ooh-a-ooh." High in a sprawling old tree, Jeff cupped his hands over his mouth and made more ape sounds. He shook a tree limb, rattling more leaves.

Michelle got off her bike and looked up toward Jeff as he began climbing out of the tree.

"It's about time, woman."

"Okay, Tarzan," Michelle laughed. "Or is it Cheetah?"

With a thud, Jeff leaped off a low branch. He made more ape gestures and sounds and laughed. He was glad to see her.

Warmly Michelle smiled. "We miss you on the outside world."

"Oh? You and who else?"

Michelle glanced down. "Your mom came to see me. . . ."

"What's she bothering you for?" Jeff questioned with annoyance.

"She thought I knew where you were. . . . She's worried."

Jeff let out a disgusted sigh.

Michelle toyed with a flower on a nearby bush. "What's she supposed to do, forget your name?" she asked half jokingly.

Abruptly Jeff changed the subject. "Come on," he grinned. "I'll show you Count Yorga's summer home."

He put his arms around Michelle's shoulders and led her into a meadow. In a distance was the sprawling, decaying mansion. From their observation point, it looked magnificent.

"Isn't there anybody around?" Michelle inquired.

"No, uh uh . . . just a weird old lady on a bike who chases butterflies!"

They both laughed. Michelle glanced at Jeff. "You look pretty strung out," she commented concernedly.

"Yeah, well . . . uh . . ." Jeff dropped her hand, and he paced on ahead of Michelle. ". . . been trying to put it all together." He turned to face her. "Everything's been up for review. Probably this is a good time to split for good." He fiddled with a tall stalk of grass. "Nothing's gonna change. . . . No matter what I do, it's never going to earn me a gold star on his performance chart!"

Michelle looked down for a moment. "Does your dad always have to set the standards?" she ventured.

Jeff threw his hand out in an exasperated gesture and gave her a frustrated stare. "Look, if you mention that Jesus stuff, I'll throw up!"

"You mentioned Him."

"Yeah, but it's written all over your face," he replied angrily. "Look, I'm tired of always feeling like you're judging me behind that Christ smile of yours because I haven't 'seen the light.' "

As if to fend off his angry words, Michelle turned her head away. "Jeff, you couldn't be more wrong. I love you," she said softly.

Unable to back down, Jeff turned away. "You just save your prayers."

"You're being pretty weird!" Michelle retorted angrily.

"You're being pretty weird yourself ... 'Mother Mary'! Reading your Bible all the time like some pious saint, all straight and proper."

Unprepared for any of this and near tears, Michelle stared at the ground, trying to reason. "Sorry if I turn you off."

"Yeah, well, I liked you better the old way."

Her voice breaking, Michelle turned away. "I'm not the old way.... I never will be again."

She began to cry, and it cooled Jeff's tirade. He hesitated for a moment, then made a stab at a half-apology.

"Hey, come on. I told you I'm going through a lot of changes . . . ," he began.

"Well, how do you think I feel when the person I love most can't understand the most important thing in my life!"

"We had a beautiful thing going," Jeff responded in a pained voice.

"Had?" Michelle said with a start.

"Well," he gestured futiley with his hands, "that slipped out . . . I . . ."

"Yeah, well, maybe it's better left past tense 'cause there's a big hole in you and every time you can't fill it, you explode against someone!"

Unable to reply, Jeff turned and stalked away. And Michelle watched him go as she cried.

☐

When the phone rang, it woke Warren up, and he leaned over to answer it. "Hello." He glanced over at Fran to see if it had wakened her, but she just stirred a little in her sleep. "Who?" He listened and then cupped his hand over his mouth and the receiver to muffle the sound. "Where,

Angie? ... Okay, look, I appreciate it. Thanks."

Slowly he got out of bed so as not to disturb Fran. He grabbed his watch and headed for the bathroom where he flicked on the light and began to dress.

At this late hour, Jeff was the only one in the laundromat. As he sat on one of the washing machines, he read a magazine and munched some crackers.

He didn't realize his dad was there until Warren stood beside him and spoke to him. "Hi."

Startled, Jeff jerked his head up. "Hi," he replied, his mouth full of crackers. He set the box of crackers down on the machine with a bang and looked back down at his magazine.

"Hey, uh, you know you're kind of a tough guy to find.... How're you doing?" Warren's voice echoed in the empty room as he walked toward Jeff.

Jeff deliberately took a swig from a bottle of cheap wine, and then he slid off the machine and yanked the washer open and began pulling his clothes out. "Oh, I'm just, uh, keepin' clean," he finally answered. With a wet "plop," he tossed the clothes into the cart and turned back to see if he had gotten everything out of the washer.

"Yeah, so I see." Warren picked up the bottle of wine and looked at it distastefully, but he said nothing.

Jeff continued to ignore him, and he began to fidget uncomfortably.

Warren's eyes rested on the box of detergent, and he picked it up and tried to make a joke. "Hey, Mr. Ecology . . . this is, uh, phosphates. . . . You know this stuff pollutes," he cracked weakly.

For a moment Jeff glared at him; then he slammed the handful of clothes into the carrier with an angry "smack" and wheeled the carrier to the dryer, keeping his back turned to Warren.

"All right, son. Look, you—you made your point. Now come on. Come on home with me, will you?"

Jeff continued to i g n o r e him. He slammed the door of the dryer and dug into his pocket for a dime.

Debating with himself, Warren took a wad of bills out of his pocket. He slipped a twenty-dollar bill of the top of the wad and stuffed it inside Jeff's jacket before he silently left.

Feeling miserable, but still unable to forgive his father, Jeff turned around and watched Warren as he walked away.

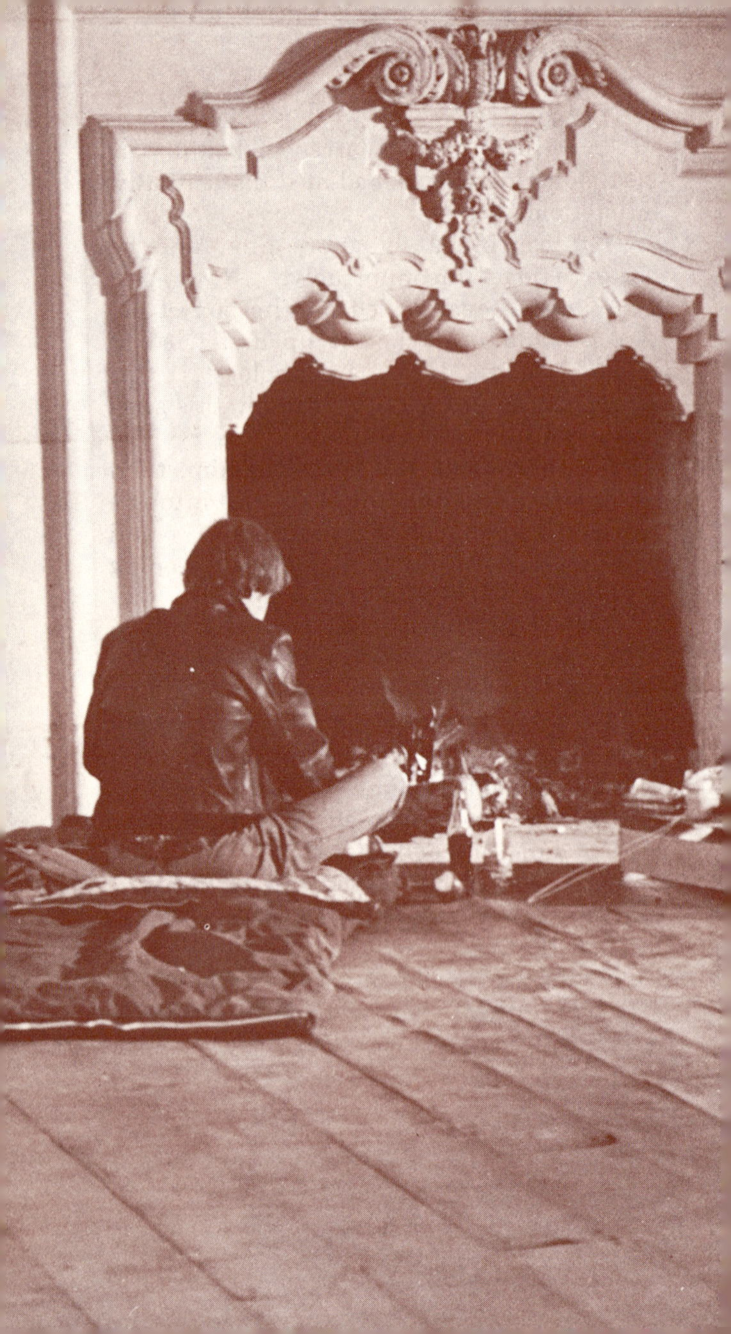

CHAPTER 6

As the old lady caretaker arrived at the wide mansion steps, her dozens of cats crawled out of their various homes to welcome her. "Come on, kitty, kitty; come on, I've got some food for you. Come, kitty."

She hurried to the patio gate and walked inside. On the patio were two old plates and a box of kittens. Two larger cats stood guard nearby and contentedly scratched in the morning sun.

"Here kitties; hello kitties. Come on, little kids. Kitty, kitty, kitty, kitty—come on, babies," she urged. She chuckled as she bent down to take a recalcitrant kitten from the box. "Hello there. Hello. Can't you get out all by yourself?"

From several directions cats began to converge as they heard the caretaker's call and as they smelled the food that was being set out for them.

"Ooh, you little baby," she cooed to the kitten as she put it down. "Here now, come on—I've got a lot of good stuff for you."

The baby kitten hesitantly tried to move into a place around the plate with the other kittens. "Aw, come on now," said the caretaker as she picked up the kitten again. "Don't you want anything to eat?" She rubbed the kitten against her cheek. "Where are the other little kitty cats?" She looked around the patio and then looked up toward the roof of the mansion.

"Ooh, they're up in the ceiling some—." She looked again. A wisp of smoke was slowly spiraling out of the chimney. The old lady paused for a moment, wondering what to do. She put the kitten down. "Now, eat your dinner. I'll be right back."

With another glance at the chimney, she hurried off, rushing out the same way she came in. She bolted through the gate and glanced up at the chimney again. Then she rushed down the steps, jumped on her bicycle and sped away.

It took half an hour for the police car to come to the mansion after the caretaker called the station. The squad continued along the road to the old house, and when it reached the entryway, the policeman turned off toward the side door where he parked the car.

Inside Jeff sat on his unrolled sleeping bag near a small fire which was flickering in the fireplace. When he heard the car door slam, he jumped up and looked out the window. Two policemen were approaching the house.

In a panic, Jeff started toward the fireplace, but there wasn't much time, so he ran out of the room. He dashed into the hallway, his shoes slipping on the marble floor as he ran. His footsteps echoed off the empty floors and walls. Jeff pulled open a door and rushed into the entrance hall. He grabbed open the front doors. A policeman was just coming up to the iron railing outside the door. Jeff slammed the door and rushed back into the house and up a stairway at the end of the hall.

The policemen ran in through the patio doors. "He's upstairs," one called to the other.

Jeff reached the top step and dashed around the corner. He tried a door. It was locked. As the policemen ran up the stairs Jeff had just climbed, he ran another direction. When he reached a double door, he kicked it open. He lost his balance and fell. Quickly scrambling to his feet, he ran through the doorway into another empty corridor. Here the draperies were tied open, exposing him in the lighted hallway.

Two more policemen entered the man-

73

sion through the front doors. They looked around; then they split up—one ran to the right and the other to the left.

As Jeff reached the other end of the corridor, two of the policemen spotted him and gave chase. He ran down the stairs which led to the servant's quarters. The policemen lost sight of him and tried the wrong door at the end of the hallway while Jeff reached the bottom of the stairs and swung himself around the corner. He opened a doorway which brought him back to the first floor entrance. Blindly he charged on. A policeman coming the other direction passed him and whirled around.

"Hey!"

Quickly Jeff charged up the stairs as the policeman, intent on catching him, dashed up after him. Jeff ran up a few nearby steps and struggled to open a large cupboard-like set of doors. As they came open, he found himself at the bottom of still another stairway. With the policemen in pursuit, he had no choice, so he ran up the stairs.

Two policemen rushed down the hall and ascended the stairs. "I saw him in here...." The other two policemen joined the first two as they all ran up the stairs.

Jeff ran through the long attic and down

the stairs on the other side. As he reached the second floor corridor, he pushed open a window and climbed onto the sill. He dropped from the window and descended an outside fire escape.

Three of the policemen ran to the open window and saw Jeff running outside. "Buzz! He's outside," shouted one as Jeff ran around the corner. He nearly collided with a policeman who grabbed his jacket. As they struggled, another policeman climbed out the window and hurried down the fire escape. Frantically, Jeff twisted and scuffled with his captor, but the other policemen caught up and piled on him.

In the police station, Fran was first to speak after their long, silent drive from home. "Warren, what are you going to say?"

"You've got to show him that you love him." She paused. "Use your heart for a change instead of that super-rational brain."

"What do you recommend, a frontal lobotomy or something?" Warren demanded sarcastically.

They entered the reception area outside lock-up and Fran held back a step as Warren grimly approached the desk.

"Yes, sir?" acknowledged an officer

as he walked over to assist them.

"Uh, we'd like to, uh, well, we've come to see our son," he replied hesitantly. He glanced nervously at Fran and began to drum on the counter with his fingers.

"The name, please."

Embarrassed, Warren answered, "Jeffrey Cole."

"Oh, right," replied the officer as he recognized Warren. "Oh, Angie!" he called to the officer behind him. Angie glanced up from his desk. "Mr. and Mrs. Cole." Angie got up and approached the counter as the reception officer looked back at Warren. "Officer Soldini will be with you in a moment, sir." He walked away from the counter as Angie came up. "Warren... Fran," he greeted them.

Fran smiled uncomfortably.

"Hi, Angie," mumbled Warren.

"Well, they got him on a misdemeanor breaking and entering."

"Oh." Warren breathed. He spread out his hands and glanced at his fingernails, not knowing what to do next. Then he reached for his checkbook. "Well, uh, is—is there some, uh—uh, charge or fine or . . .?" he began to question.

"Oh—no, no, that'll all come later," explained Angie. "I mean, restitution should only run in the neighborhood of—fifty bucks."

"Okay, thank—thanks, Angie," Warren replied as Jeff was ushered into the room.

Jeff called out to the officer stationed by the door, "Check you later, Harvey." Slowly he walked over to Fran and Warren. He attempted to cover his discomforture with some jokes. "You know, they really take lousy pictures in there . . ." He held up his fingers. "But I did a great job on the prints!"

Warren did not smile, and Jeff slinked past him to his mother. As Fran turned to leave, Jeff put his arm around her shoulders.

□

Bitterly and frustratedly, Warren pounded his fingers on the counter, the words pushing against his teeth, rejecting all of them. Then, resigned, he turned and left the room.

"Thanks," began Jeff as he walked into the living room. Warren flicked on the light and gave him a small laugh of dismissal. "We're not interested in punishing you for some exotic crime . . ."

"I'll pay back that fifty dollars," Jeff responded.

"No hurry."

Jeff plopped down on the sofa, and the room was silent until Fran came in.

"Yeah," Warren began again, "I guess you're kind of tired from your—jail experience, huh?"

As she took off her coat, Fran tensed a bit. "How about a fresh start in the morning?"

Jeff replied. "I'm not afraid to talk about it, really.... I just want you to know that I'm sorry I put you to all this trouble."

"Forget it," Warren answered.

"We'd all better get some sleep," Fran suggested.

Jeff tried to be casual. "I must have really put you through the wringer."

"Well, it was worth it," Warren responded in a charitable tone. "At least you knew you were wrong, son." He patted Jeff on the head.

As these last words sank in Jeff challenged, "About what?"

Warren walked into the den as he continued. "Well, your emotional accusations on television—I suppose that's where it started." He paused. "I'm sure you got something out of Dave's lecture—at least about our safety factors!"

Jeff got up from the sofa. "You must

keep pretty heavy surveillance down there, Daddy," he replied sarcastically.

Warren began to explain. "Oh, look, I just happened to cas—." He broke off as Jeff glared at him. "Somehow this superrational brain of mine can't penetrate that *particular* tone of voice!" he flared.

"I didn't say I was wrong—I said I was sorry," explained Jeff.

Fran looked at Jeff and then at Warren. "Will you both stop behaving like spoiled brats—," she began.

"Fran, stay out of this," Warren interrupted sharply. His hands were on his hips and he continued to scowl at Jeff.

Angrily, Fran jumped up. "What *am* I—some kind of a gadget you can turn on and off when you want dinner or . . ."

Warren pointed his finger at her. "Look, I told you to leave us alone . . ."

As they glared at each other, Jeff jumped up. "Why don't you leave her alone?" He raised his voice. "You've been doing this big father number on me for the last couple of years. Well, I can take it. Just leave her alone!" Jeff turned and dashed out of the room.

"Wait a minute, pal. . . ," Warren shouted.

Jeff whirled around in the doorway. "No,

79

you just wait a minute! You can talk to my probation officer!" For a moment, Jeff's words hung suspended in the air. Then he turned. "I'll sleep in the van."

Now Fran was galvanized into action, and she dashed after Jeff. "Jeff!" she pleaded.

As righteous outrage began to take over, Fran turned to Warren. "When is somebody in this house going to love somebody!" Jeff turned away. "Is that so difficult, Warren?" she demanded.

Warren's mouth clamped shut, and he turned on his heel and abruptly left the hall. Fran turned to Jeff as he started to head for the front door. She took a menacing step forward. "And you—upstairs!" Deciding this was not the time to tangle with his mother, Jeff slouched upstairs.

Her hot anger still flaring, Fran stood there a second. Then she cooled off. All that was left was hurt—bone deep hurt.

Warren paced the den; then he slid open the sliding glass doors and walked outside. With his hands in his pockets, he continued pacing, his adrenalin kicking at his frustration. He gazed at Jeff's window as he saw the light go on in his room.

Aimlessly Jeff wandered around his room. Still upset, he walked into the bathroom and flicked on the light. Then he turned on the water in the tub.

Warren watched through the glass door as Fran entered the den. Stubbornly, he debated with himself, but he wouldn't go inside.

Feeling dejected and miserably alone and unaware that Warren was watching her, Fran settled wearily onto the sofa and bowed her head.

Warren pulled open the sliding door. Fran remained huddled on the sofa, then looked up as he came inside. He walked to his desk and began fiddling with his pencil holder—the one Jeff had made in third grade. "Well, I tried, I really tried," he sighed.

"The effort was not exactly noticeable," Fran responded as Warren loosened his tie without comment. "You win!" Fran seethed. She studied Warren with cold objectivity. "That's what counts, doesn't it? You just have to win. You're playing some kind of computerized chess game—it's fixed so that you always come out on top." She bit her fist to keep from saying more.

Warren walked over and sat down beside her. He put his hands over hers. "You know I love you, Honey." Fran turned her head

81

away as he traced a pattern on his wrist. "It's the job, Fran...," he explained. "I know we're all drifting away from each other... and as soon as we pass the critical stage at the plant, I promise you—"

"What about the critical stage here?" Fran interrupted.

For a moment her question stopped him, and Warren tried to find words to soothe their estrangement. "It's the same thing. You see, don't you, Honey?" he implored.

Fran began to brim over as her eyes filled with tears. "Warren, there's — there's got to be a stop. Things keep building up and driving us further and further apart." The admission of her torment pulled the plug, and the tears spilled out.

Warren gripped her hand. "I promise you—I'll make it right, I promise! I—I just need a little more time."

As far as Fran was concerned there was no more time. She continued to weep as Warren sat helplessly watching her.

One more time... thought Warren as he went up the stairs and entered Jeff's room. "Jeff..." Getting no reply, he glanced around the room, and as he heard water running in the bathtub he went into the bathroom. "Jeff, I..." Something was wrong! Warren looked inside the shower curtain. Jeff had disappeared again. Defeated, Warren turned off the running water and pulled the plug.

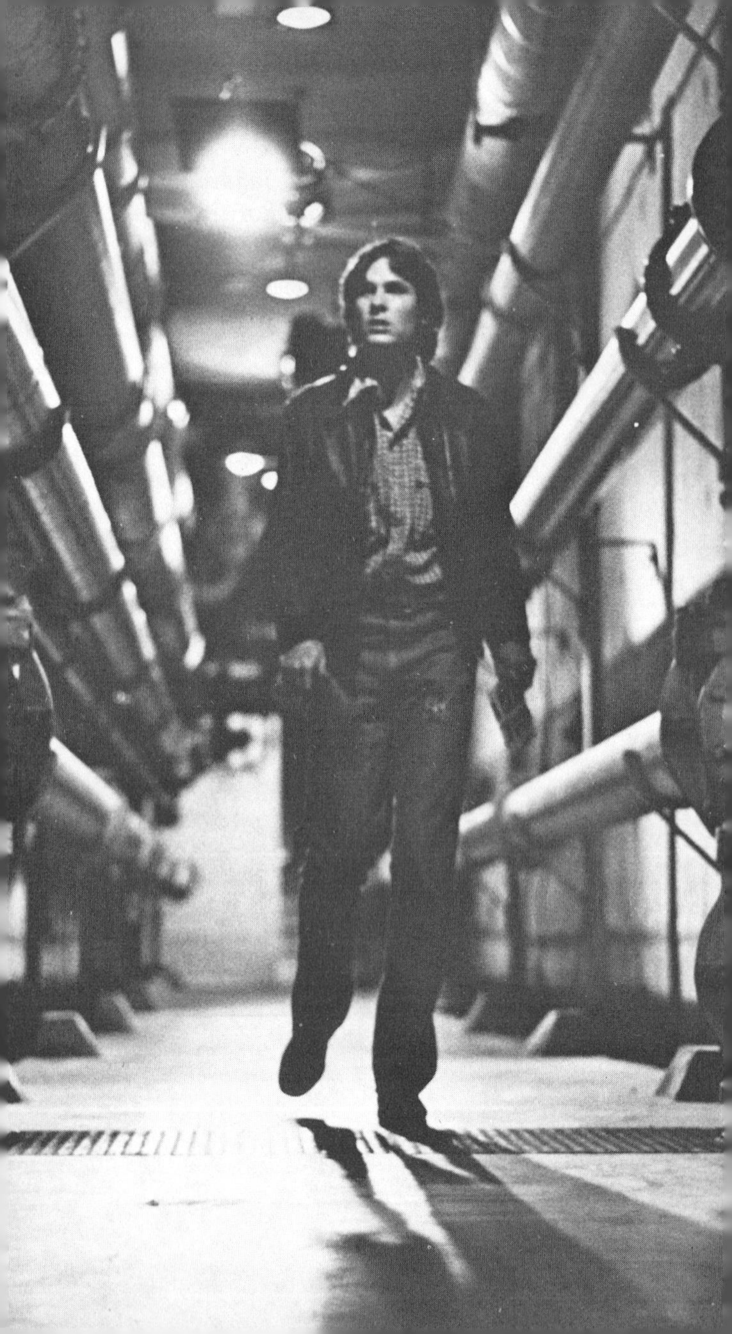

CHAPTER 7

The fountain outside the FAEMAD reception area chugged laboriously as soap bubbles billowed out of the pulsating water. When the gate guard made his hourly check he noticed it. He quickly entered a station and picked up the telephone.

In the FAEMAD Security Systems, a guard answered his ring.

"Security," called the gate guard. "We've got some monkey business at the fountain. Can you pick up anything?"

"We'll get right on it," he responded as he punched a button on the monitor system and focused in on the fountain area. "And maybe you'd better call Warren Cole," he advised before the gate guard hung up.

The gate guard glanced out at the fountain as bubbles continued to billow over the sides. "Mr. Cole, I'm sorry to disturb you, but we have a possible entry at the plant," he called into the phone.

The night guard in Security Systems got

on the intercom to warn the other guards. "We are alerting all units to a possible illegal entry of the south." He looked at the Security Systems map which had lights designating each area. The light in Area 1, the entrance, was lit up and glowing red. As the light switched to the "By-Pass Station" area, the night guard called to the security guard, "Scan By-Pass area." As the closed circuit picture centered on the By-Pass area, a small figure of someone running could be seen. "There he is!" the guard exclaimed into the phone.

"Unit Four," called the night guard, "check out By-Pass area for illegal entry."

Jeff ran across the By-Pass area to an open space beside a tall building. He ducked under the chain which blocked off the stairway; then he turned and slapped a sticker on the "By-Pass" plaque which hung from the chain. The sticker read, "EARTH—NO DEPOSIT, NO RETURN." Jeff ran down the stairs.

As two security guards looked around, one shined his flashlight on the ecology sticker left by Jeff.

"Hey, Bob, look at this . . ."

"We'd better call in," responded the other guard, "Looks like he's gone below."

Jeff ran through the By-Pass area, pausing every once in awhile to place a sticker on the long pipes which lined the walls. He stuck a sticker on one of the pipe elbows and stood back to admire his handiwork. Looking around for something else to do, Jeff spotted the meter box at one side. The lights on it were glowing bright green. Jeff flipped both of the levers down, turned a dial and pushed several of the buttons.

Suddenly the guards appeared at the end of the By-pass corridor; their flashlights beamed down the long area like headlights. Jeff darted up a nearby ladder as the guards ran to the meter box. They quickly returned the lever, dials and buttons to their normal position as Jeff reached the top of the ladder and ran up some nearby stairs.

The night guard was on the phone again talking with Warren. "Yes, Mr. Cole. Well, uh, we had him in By-Pass, but, uh, we lost him."

Warren talked agitatedly into his car phone. "Well, you'd better find out who it is by the time I get there, or I'll be lopping off some heads!"

Jeff moved nimbly along a catwalk and swung around a corner and streaked down some stairs.

The two guards at the beginning of the

catwalk didn't know which way to go. The guard's voice echoed as he shouted, "He's outside!" They each went a different direction onto the roof outside.

Jeff continued running, and as he passed another stairway he turned back and decided to go down it. He ran through the doorway to another door which had "Electrical Relay" printed on it. As he got inside the room, he scanned it. He pulled a can of black spray paint out of his pocket and sprayed the faces of the meters and gauges, turning dials at the same time. Then he opened a cabinet full of colored wires and sprayed them also.

As soon as Jeff entered the room, the red light for "Electrical Relay" began flashing on the FAEMAD map.

"All units report to Electrical Relay immediately. Possible sabotage," warned the night guard.

Jeff finished spraying the wires and closed the cabinet and ran back down the corridor. He climbed the stairs at the end of the hall and ran through the upstairs corridor. After looking both right and left, Jeff grabbed open an unmarked door and ran inside.

This was the same room where Dave Green had begun his class lecture a few days before. Closing the door quietly behind,

Jeff tiptoed into the room. He peeked cautiously in the window of Master Control. Inside Master Control, a white-coated technician was making some adjustments at the computer panel. Jeff crouched beneath the window and crossed under it. When he was safely past the view from the window, he stood up and tiptoed into the Conference Room and pushed the door shut behind him.

For a moment Jeff watched the technician through the Conference Room window; then he set his paint can on the table and glanced around.

Warren burst into Security Systems. "All right, let's have it. You find him?"

"No, sir."

There was an awkward moment as they all stared at one another. Then Warren leaned toward the control panel. "Then let's seal off the building."

A red light went on above the door, indicating that it was locked, and they continued pushing buttons to lock up the entire complex.

The Conference Room door locked with a loud "snap." As the red light went on, Jeff dashed for the door and tried to pull it open, but it was too late. Caught, he winced and waited.

Warren stood behind the guards who

were seated at the screen. "Well, what have we got, Fred?"

"I can't seem to pinpoint it," the guard replied.

Impatiently, Warren grumbled, "Let's go, let's go!"

Suddenly one of the guards at the console called to Warren. "Mr. Cole..."

"Yeah..." Warren turned back to him.

"We've got him in the Conference Room."

Warren watched the screen. His face was lined and creased as he attempted to comprehend what he saw. The closed circuit camera zoomed in for a closeup of Jeff. He paced the floor; then, as he noticed the camera's eye on him, his lips moved in a wordless obscenity.

In disbelief, Warren and the guards looked at the screen. The Security Systems door opened as Dave put his card in the slot. He looked at the screen, and, as he recognized Jeff, he closed his mouth and didn't say a word.

Warren snapped off the picture and turned away. Embarrassed, none of the others made a move. After taking a moment to regain his composure, Warren asked the guard to release the locks on the building. In a kind of silent "thank you" Warren put his hand on the night guard's shoulder. Resignedly, he walked out and toward the Conference Room.

Jeff sat at the end of the table with his feet propped up on it. Without turning on the light, Warren entered the room and closed the door. For a moment, they silently stared in the darkness. And, with an insolent expression on his face, Jeff waited for his father to speak.

Jeff frowned and began, "Uh, how's this for a headline, 'Father Traps Son in Sabotage Plot.'"

Warren flicked on the light switch.

"Hey, I'd make a great P.R. man," Jeff continued. "You might even make the tube again!"

"Why do you always have to say something like that," charged Warren, "that doesn't relate to anything?" When all he received for a reply was stony silence, he gestured in frustration. "All I see is hate —I mean, you for me!"

Jeff continued to stare at Warren.

"I don't know, maybe—," Warren pondered, "maybe I did something that makes you feel that way—."

"Uh, no diversionary tactics, okay," Jeff countered. As he talked, he stood up and began to pace. "I came here to foul up your toy!"

"Oh, Jeff, come on—this 'toy' has so

many automatic systems built in, you could never be any more than—an annoyance." Baffled, Warren sat down and continued, "I mean, all—all this energy!"

Jeff kept on staring at Warren silently.

"Why can't you see that every dream I ever had will all come back to you...."

"That's it!" Jeff interrupted with a shout. "They've always been yours!"

Warren began to protest, but Jeff's words cut him off.

"Look, you gave up on me when I blew algebra!"

The words had a ring of truth, and Warren stared at Jeff, who, seeing that he'd gotten through to his father, turned away, shaken.

Warren groped for words. "I...I don't know...I try..." He sighed. "Everything you ever asked for...I gave you...I don't know anymore...I'm afraid."

Warren had never before admitted any self-doubt to his son, and Jeff struggled with his feelings. Warren's head was bowed; he felt helpless.

□

Dave moved quickly from one panel to another in Master Control. His voice interrupted the silence in the Conference Room as he called over the speaker. "Warren, the terminal generator just reported electrical failure. They're losing power," he continued more urgently, "and we're close to a critical overload." The lights went dim.

Still caught in the emotion of his confession and in the involvement of his crisis with Jeff, Warren was unaware of the outside crisis for the moment.

"I want to . . . ," began Jeff.

Dave knocked sharply on the window, his mouth forming "Warren!"

"I just want to be free of you!"

Warren jerked his head up so he faced Jeff; then he noticed the lights dimming again. Dave knocked on the window again.

"Your dreams . . . plans for me . . . ," Jeff went on.

Distracted, Warren began to respond to the emergency in Master Control. The lights dimmed again.

With a feeble plea, Jeff called, "Dad . . ."

As if forgetting Jeff's presence, Warren jumped up and hurried toward the door.

"Dad . . ." Jeff turned away, furious with himself for almost believing that his father cared! The door closed behind Warren as he rushed into Master Control.

93

He hurried over to the computer panel as the lights dimmed again.

"We're fluctuating between sixty and a hundred," Dave explained.

Warren stuffed the printout the technician was holding. "These limits aren't going to hold!" He turned to the technician. "Alert the local sub-stations. We're switching to backup." Warren turned to the computer programmer and began pushing buttons. He reached over to the master panel and shouted to Dave. "Okay, I'm going to kill 'A.'"

"Right." Dave responded by flipping two switches.

As he read numbers, Warren mumbled to himself and scurried around making adjustments. "Seven, six, three, nine . . ."

"No, no," responded the technician, "we won't be able to hold at that."

"Seven, six, three, nine, seven," Warren continued as Dave watched the gauge.

The technician continued speaking into the phone. "We're running a computer check at the present time. . . . The problem should be corrected in a matter of seconds."

Warren finished punching the combination and crossed back to the programmer. "Okay, I'm going to reactivate 'A.' Tell them to stand by for a surge," he told the technician.

As Warren punched a button, the panel lighted up again.

The technician went on speaking into the phone, "Okay, stand by for a surge. They're taking the By-Pass system off..." He looked at Dave. "How's she read?"

For a moment Dave watched the gauge; then he flipped the two switches back on. "Good. We're holding steady." "Okay."

"There might be a slight rise in the voltage for five or ten seconds," the technician explained into the phone.

Warren pointed to the printout panel. "Dave, you want to record these for retrieval?"

Dave rushed over to the panel. "I'll handle it."

Warren turned to the technician. "Tell them the conversion is holding complete."

"The conversion is holding complete," repeated the technician.

Warren hovered for a second. Then, when he was certain everything was under control, he walked back to the Conference Room. He let himself in with his security card. Jeff was gone! The opportunity was lost. Slowly Warren walked into the room and sat down at the table.

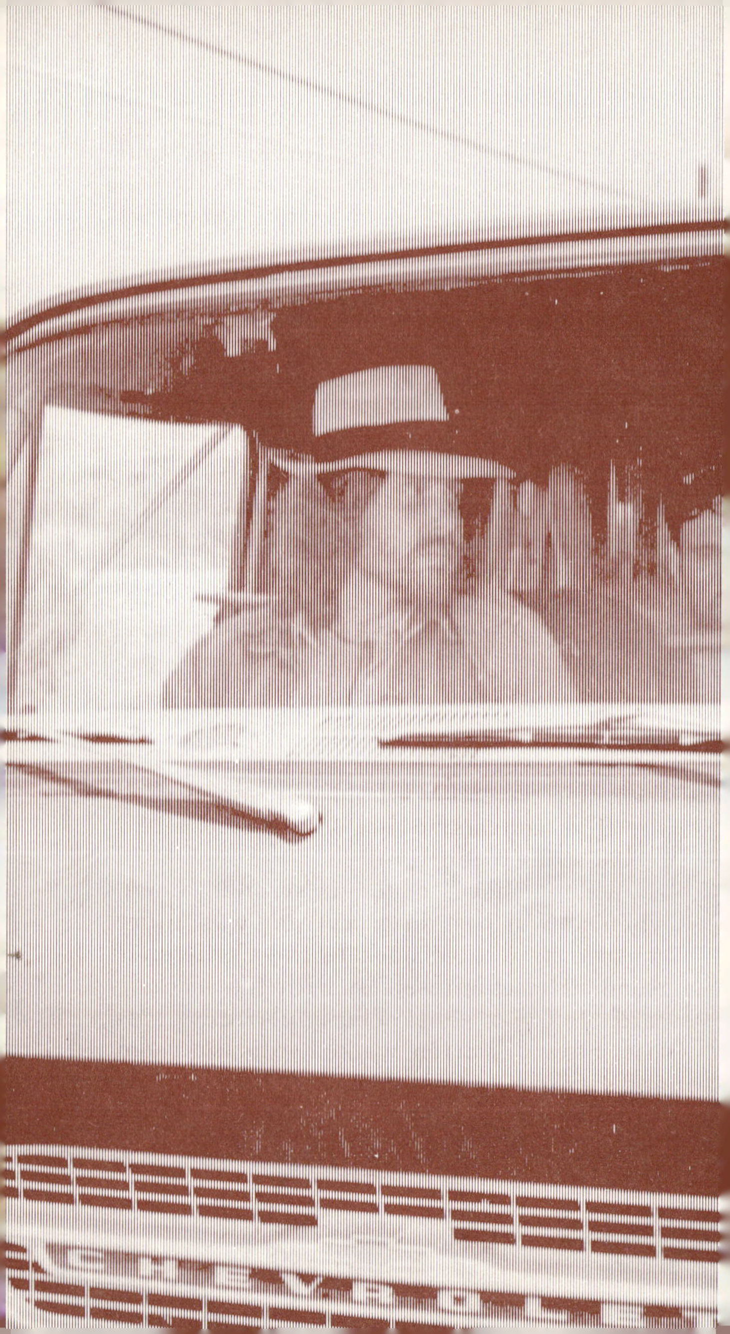

CHAPTER 8

Jeff's van moved along the highway. As he noticed a traveler with a backpack walking ahead alongside the road, he pulled over and slowed down.

"Hey, need a lift?" he called out the window.

The hitchhiker grinned gratefully and rushed to the van as Jeff came to a complete step. "Thanks alot!" He pulled open the door and shoved his backpack in. As he settled into the seat beside Jeff, Jeff tossed his backpack into the back of the truck. "Never fails. Every time I hear a car, I just start walkin'!"

Jeff smiled over at him. "Where you headed?"

"Just travelin'. You?"

"Oh, no place particular," Jeff replied. "Just—away."

"That's cool." The traveler eyed Jeff. "Just splittin,' huh?"

"Yeah," Jeff replied absently. As the words sank in, he looked closely at his rider. "Yeah," he said with a definite emphasis.

The rider began setting out food on the dashboard... a jar of baby food, a couple of bags of dried fruit. "Hey, listen, you hungry?"

Dubiously, Jeff eyed the food. His eyes settled on the jar of strained peaches. "Uh, nah, not really," he decided.

"Hey, man, it's rip-off time. You take what you can get."

Jeff squinted his eyes and, feeling uncomfortable, he glanced at the traveler.

"Wait'll you have to live for a week on just dog biscuits!" the rider continued. "'Course you don't get any blue chip stamps!" he grinned. Then he pulled a beer out of his knapsack and handed it to Jeff. Jeff accepted it gratefully.

"Hey, thanks."

"Sure."

Jeff pulled the snap top, and beer spurted out. The traveler jumped back.

"Woe!" Jeff laughed in surprise, and the traveler joined him.

"First time on the road?" he inquired.

"Yeah... just about," replied Jeff as he sipped his beer.

"I've been movin' around about three years now..."

"Umm!" Jeff was impressed.

The hitchhiker began to eat the baby food. "Been all over the States, Canada, Alaska, Europe twice, Africa..."

"Africa!" Jeff exclaimed incredulously.

"Yeah... you ever see a whole country three feet off the ground?"

Jeff's glance was uncomfortable.

"You oughta go to Morocco, Man," the traveler continued. "Talk about grass... over there's kief, hash, anything you want. It's like buying bubble gum."

Jeff didn't reply, and the silence was broken only by the sound of the van's motor and the music coming from the tape deck.

The van continued down the narrow road and around a curve. Another van was pulled off the road at an angle. Jeff leaned forward in his seat to look at the vehicle, and as he approached it, he honked his horn. As they got closer, Jeff honked again. It was a "Jesus van." Written on top in huge red letters was "JESUS." A couple of kids were changing a tire. The traveler whistled at them as the van passed. Then he turned to Jeff. "Jesus freaks. Always good for a place to crash." He took off his hat and pulled something out of the inner band. "Always there with the goodies," he continued. He put the hat back on his head.

"Really?" asked Jeff.

"Yeah," replied the rider as he put a reefer into his mouth and lit it. He had a few more stored in the band of his hat. "They get off on Jesus like He was grass." He handed the joint to Jeff. With a shrug, he took the cigarette. "Tie in with them every chance you get," suggested the traveler. "The magic words are 'Praise the Lord' and 'Pass the mashed potatoes!'"

□

With her mind far away, Fran pushed her shopping cart down the supermarket aisle. As she opened the dairy case, she automatically took out two half-gallons of milk; then the realization hit that she was shopping for only two. Halfheartedly Fran replaced one carton in the dairy case. Her interest in shopping faded as she headed back down the aisle.

□

Warren drifted aimlessly through Master Control with his coat tossed over one shoulder. He punched a printout button and read the figures for awhile. He turned to Dave who was sitting at the console, immersed in his work. Feeling like a fifth wheel, Warren switched off the print-out machine. He shrugged on his coat and left the room.

□

As Jeff's van moved down the highway, the hitchhiker's head rolled with the van's motion as he slept against the back of the seat. Suddenly the van began bumping, and Jeff pulled to a stop at the side of the road. The traveler woke as Jeff mumbled, "Feels like a flat."

Jeff climbed out and walked around the van, checking the tires. The right rear tire was indeed very flat! He opened the back of the van and leaned inside to get the spare. "Yeah, it's a flat," he called to the traveler.

"You need any help?"

"Yeah." Jeff pulled out the spare. "The jack and tire tool are right under the seat."

"Okay." The hitchhiker got the tools while Jeff bounced the spare. He handed the tools to Jeff. Then he stood and watched him.

A station wagon came along, and, in the time-honored tradition, the traveler wagged his thumb. When the wagon stopped, the hitchhiker dashed to get his backpack out of the van. He hesitated when Jeff didn't look up. "I—I got a ride...," he explained.

"Huh?" Jeff said without looking up.

"I got a ride," the traveler repeated.

"Oh." Jeff was disappointed, and it showed on his face.

"See you, man." The traveler was eager to be off. "Take care, huh?" He ran toward the station wagon.

"Yeah," Jeff replied as he squatted by the flat tire.

As the station wagon took off, Jeff tossed the crowbar onto the ground and looked up. He was completely alone.

□

Fran walked out of the supermarket with her sackful of groceries. As she unlocked her car and set the groceries inside, she glanced through the windows across the street. There stood a picturesque little church. As if drawn by an unseen force, she crossed the street and walked inside the sanctuary. She wandered down the aisle past colorful stained glass windows. Finally, she sank into a pew. Her emotions spilled over, and she began to weep.

□

Jeff sat on the flat tire while he tightened the lug nuts on the spare. When he finished, he put the flat in the van, and he was on his way again.

□

Fran pulled into the driveway and took the groceries out of the back seat. As she carried them to the kitchen door, Warren came to meet her.

He took the groceries from her. "Hi, Honey."

"What's happened . . . is it Jeff?" she questioned with a dismayed look on her face.

"Oh, no, no," Warren replied as he carried the groceries into the kitchen.

"Well, have you heard from him?" she persisted.

"No." Warren set the groceries on the counter. "Just thought I'd kinda hang around home today, you know, kinda break the pattern." He fidgeted while Fran took some ground sirloin from the sack and opened the refrigerator.

"You realize we haven't had a vacation in five years?" he continued, but Fran didn't turn around. "We're both a little too old for an identity crisis, but . . . we could consider a holiday."

Fran slammed the refrigerator door. "A holiday?" she declared in a startled voice.

"Yeah, Europe, or South America... maybe, wherever you want to go," Warren finished.

Angrily Fran turned to face him. "Only *you* could come up with something like this!"

"Like what?" Warren did not understand.

"We have no idea where Jeff is, and you have us off on some vacation! It's incredible, Warren, really incredible." Fran turned and left the room.

He followed her. "Fran..."

She rushed into the entry hall and up the stairs.

"Fran, please...!" He continued calling her from the bottom of the stairs. The tone of his voice stopped her. "Fran... I always believed that growth was the most important factor in life to—to achieve as much actualization of one's potential as possible." His eyes began filling, and his voice was soft. "And somehow I — I over-achieved, at least with Jeff and..."

Warren's honesty softened her anger, and Fran turned to look at him.

He paused, and she turned her head

away. A deep sigh escaped as he realized he was not getting through. He gestured helplessly and tried again. "What I'm trying to say is I ... don't want to lose you ..."

Fran faced him again, her anger gone, replaced by pain and confusion.

"Is it possible to go back, Fran, to— to fill in the silences?"

As tears filled her eyes, Fran sat down on the stairs.

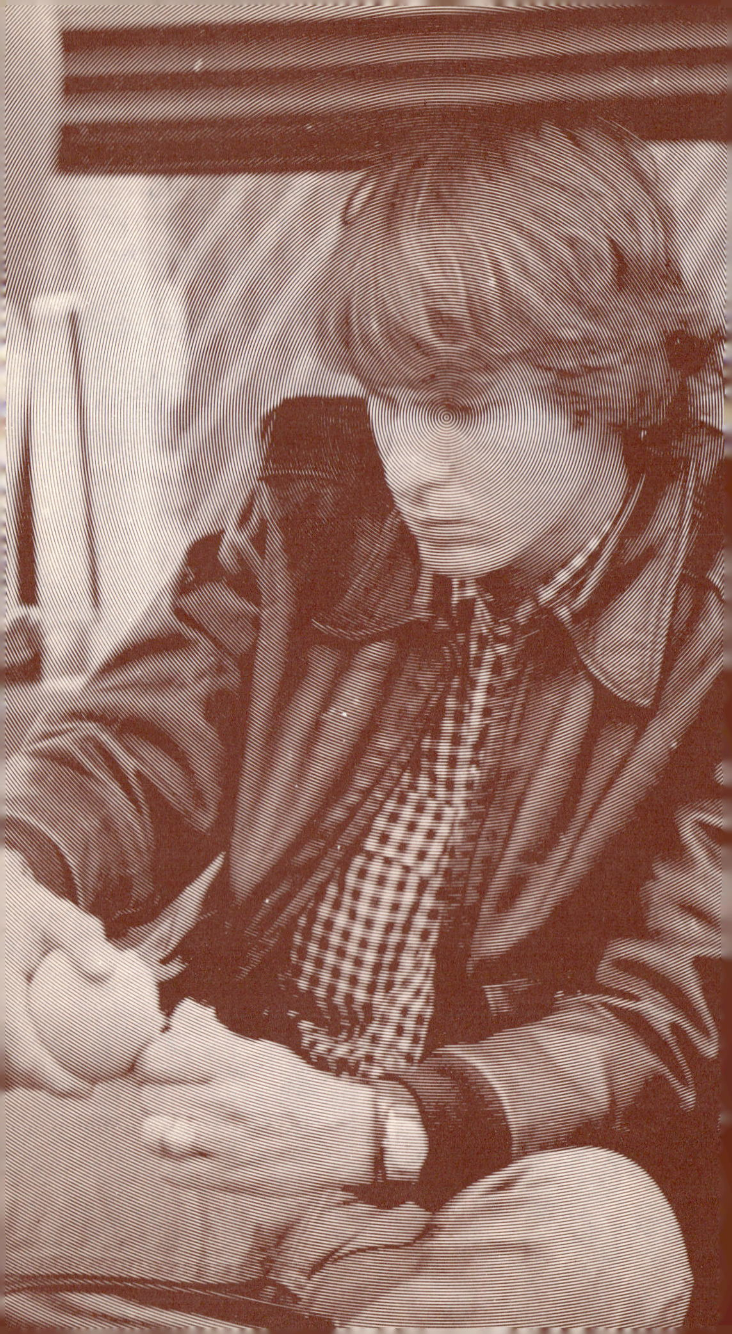

CHAPTER 9

It was dawn, and the gas-station owner began to open up for the day. He had a tiny shabby station with two pumps and a shack-like garage out in the middle of nowhere. As the owner walked to his pumps, he spied the parked van.

He walked over and peered inside; then he banged on the window to wake up Jeff.

Mumbling, Jeff pushed open the doors. "Mornin'."

Not sure whether or not he was in trouble, Jeff replied, "Morning." Then, almost automatically he said, "Fill 'er up!"

"Got any money?"

Jeff checked his wallet. "Uh, better make it three bucks."

The owner nodded and began tending his pumps, still keeping an eye on Jeff. Jeff began pulling on his boots.

"Got a pot of coffee on inside," the owner invited.

"Hey, thanks." Jeff finished pulling on his boots. His day was a little brighter.

Aimlessly he drove his van down the highway. At an intersection he noticed a hitchhiking couple standing alongside the road just beyond the stoplights. As Jeff pulled over, the couple ran toward him. He smiled a small greeting.

Rob and Patti rushed to get into the van. Rob pulled the door open. "Hey, thanks a lot, man."

"Yeah, hop in." Jeff threw his jacket into the back so there would be more room.

Patti settled into the middle beside him. "Are you going into the city?"

"Well," Jeff answered, "if it's up ahead, I guess I am."

Rob pulled the door shut. "We really prayed you'd stop."

Inwardly Jeff grimaced as he pulled the van back onto the highway.

"How's your day been goin'?" asked Rob.

"Oh, just movin' along."

"We sure didn't plan on being stranded back there," said Patti.

"Nah. We're trying to make it to the Sports Arena," Rob explained. "Billy Graham's there."

When he heard the name, Jeff's jaw tightened up a little.

"It's the Lord's timing," Patti concluded. "He knows best."

Rob nodded in agreement.

"Well, maybe you're not missing very much," Jeff countered. "Graham probably, uh, repeats himself a lot."

Rob and Patti looked at each other and laughed. Jeff glanced at the couple and grinned. A rapport had been established. For several miles they continued in lively conversation.

Jeff frowned, for he was deep in thought. "I don't know, I just can't believe in a God that would allow war, and napalm, and starving kids, for instance."

"When we turn our backs on His Son . . . man, you can see the results," replied Rob.

"You mean people decide to choose God . . . ," Jeff groped for words; "they'll uh, automatically change overnight and everybody'll live happily ever after?" He grinned cynically.

"Well, you know, God wants to change our hearts," said Rob. "But He won't back you into a corner with no way out, 'cause that's not love."

Jeff reached the parking lot entrance. A sea of cars was parked in the lot adjacent to the Sports Arena. The meeting had begun, and Billy Graham's voice was booming over the loudspeakers.

"Thanks, Jeff." Patti smiled.

"You're welcome. . . . Well, you better hurry up, the big man's doing his thing."

As they jumped out, Rob yelled back into the van, "Why don't you come on in with us?"

"Ahh, no thanks." Jeff's negative reaction was immediate and obvious.

"Why'd you go so far out of your way to get us here?"

"I . . . used to know a girl . . . that'd be turned on by Graham. I guess it was for her," Jeff explained.

Rob's smile was understanding. He and Patti turned to leave.

"The Lord loves you, Jeff," she said softly as they ran off.

A twinge of loneliness moved through Jeff as he watched them go off hand in hand. Before they turned a corner, Patti looked back and waved at him. He casually returned the wave and drove on through the parking lot.

Billy Graham's voice continued over the

loudspeaker. "Simon and Garfunkel wrote this:

'Impaled upon my wall, my eyes dimly see,
The pattern of my life and
the puzzle that is me.' "

The familiar words of the song being quoted grabbed Jeff's attention, and he pulled up by the WPQ-TV sound truck and stopped to listen.

"From the moment of my birth
To the instant of my death,
There are patterns I must follow
Just as I must breathe each breath.
Like a rat in a maze
The path before me lies,
And the pattern never alters
Until the rat dies."

Jeff turned off his engine and continued to listen.

"Is that the way your life seems? Just a circle? Just a maze—no purpose and no meaning, life makes no sense? Did you know that you can really live any way that you want to live . . . and there's nothing God can do about it?" As Mr. Graham spoke, the people inside the Sports Arena listened intently.

"You're not a puppet on a string; you're not a mechanical toy that God winds up and turns you loose and you do what you're supposed to do. You're made in the image of God—you're made in the moral image of God—you can choose!"

Now Jeff was really listening.

"You can choose the kind of life you're going to lead. If you want to lead a life totally away from God, pleasing your own flesh, your own desires, under the control of your own will without any restraints, without any Lordship of Jesus Christ, go ahead and do it!" As Billy Graham spoke, he held up his Bible and faced each side of the arena.

"No, you cannot escape Jesus. You can try, but you can't do it. If Jesus claimed to be God knowing that He was not, then, of course, He's a liar. If Jesus thought He was God and didn't know the difference, He was a maniac. But if Jesus Christ is who He claims to be, God in the flesh, then nothing else counts except to know Him. With all of our scientific and technological achievements, with all of our intellectualism, we cannot escape Jesus."

Jeff opened his glove compartment and took out an orange. He opened the door to be more comfortable and settled back to listen.

"Everybody has to decide about Jesus. Who is He? What was He? What demands does He have on my life today? God said, 'I'll become a man!'

"And young people, I want to tell you, that's who Jesus Christ is! God became a man! And God in the form of Jesus Christ, born of a virgin, walked among us, and He showed us what God is like. And if you want to know what God is like, I suggest you take a long look at Jesus."

Jeff began peeling his orange; his mind was intent on what Billy Graham was saying.

"I watch Him as He makes the blind man to see and the dumb man to talk and the dead man to rise. But that wasn't why He came. He didn't come just to live among us; He didn't come just to teach us a new way of life. Jesus Christ came for another purpose—He came to die on the cross.

"You see, the cross of Christ where He died for our sins, that was judgment. Jesus said, 'To this end I was born.' He was not accidently put to death. And He said, 'My God, why hast Thou forsaken Me?' At that moment, in some mysterious way,

God was judging His Son instead of us. He didn't just give Him to die; He gave Him to sin. He became sin for us!"

The TV cameraman focused their cameras on Mr. Graham.

"The Bible says, 'All have sinned.' What does 'sin' mean? Sin means that you've broken the law of God. Sin means that you've come short of God's holy requirements for eternal life. All of us are sinners. All of us have missed the mark."

□

In the Coles' den, Fran sat with a cup of coffee in her hands. She was watching the meeting from the Sports Arena on TV.

From outside, Warren called to her. "Honey, I was just going through my bag. I can't find my nine iron or my putter." He came into the den carrying his golf bag.

"I think they might be in Jeff's room—he used them last summer." Fran turned her attention back to the television.

"Sin builds a barrier between God and man, and sin can be conquered only by Jesus Christ. That's why He came and died on the cross, to conquer sin, to take away this cosmic loneliness that we all feel."

As Warren saw what Fran was watching, he put down his golf bag and walked over beside her.

"You know," Mr. Graham continued, "the God of the Bible is not some cold, impersonal formula or some power..."

Fran turned to Warren. "You want some coffee?"

"Yeah, um-humm." Warren sat down with his feet on the coffee table, his eyes focused on the television.

"... that's off there in space. Jesus said, 'I've come to bring life and life abundantly!' Jesus said you cannot serve God and Mammon."

As Warren listened, he absent-mindedly pulled on the fingers of his golf glove.

"He said, 'A man's life consisteth not in the abundance of the things that he possesses.' Riches make people solitary, lonely and often afraid.

"If you make money your God, it leaves you empty. George Bernard Shaw said, 'There are two tragedies in life: one is not to get your heart's desire. And the other is to get it.'

"You think if you had a lot of money you'd be happy. Some of you have already got a lot, and you're not happy.

"Two tragedies—you didn't get it, and you did get it. You see, without God, life

115

loses its zest and its purpose and its meaning. You were made for God..."

□

Jeff continued eating his orange, his mind on the sound from the loudspeaker.

"... and without God, you can never find total fulfillment..."

□

"Oh, thanks," Warren said as Fran handed him a mug of coffee.

"... and total satisfaction. How many people are watching me that are having problems in your home? He can give you a new home."

Mr. Graham's words hit the nail on the head for Fran, and, before her eyes returned to the TV screen, she shot a quick glance at Warren.

"Turn it over to Him; take all the selfishness out, and put Christ first and see what happens. What is the cure? The cure is Christ, to go to our knees."

Warren was completely absorbed in that which Billy Graham was saying. "If you wait until you can understand it all or accept it all scientifically, you'll never come.

"Jesus said, 'Except you become as a little child and be converted, you cannot enter the Kingdom of Heaven.' What does 'converted' mean? Converted just means change. You're going in one direction in your life, and you change and start a new direction, and your new direction is toward God. With Christ in your heart, that's conversion."

☐

Jeff licked the juice from the orange off his hands and stretched a little.

"Conversion is the work of God. All you have to do is be willing, and He'll do it. I'm going to ask you to submit and surrender your life and your heart to Him and start life all over again—with His love and His power to help you.

"What do you have to do? You have to be willing to give up your sin and confess that you've failed and sinned against God. I'm going to ask you by faith to come to His cross where He shed His blood for you, and let Him wash you clean of your past and change your life and make you a new person. I'm asking you to get up out of your seat and come and stand right here in front of the platform and say 'I want Christ; I choose Christ as my Lord and my Master and my Saviour.' "

As Mr. Graham concluded his message,

people left their seats and came to the front of the platform. There were teenagers and younger children. Some came by themselves. There were older people; husbands and wives walked forward together, and individuals came.

"There's a young man, there's a young woman, there's a father, there's a mother here tonight that Christ is speaking to."

As the people streamed forward, the area in front of the platform was filled with people.

"And you're going to have to face death and you're going to have the face the Judgment. And you're going to have to face life. And you really can't face anything without Christ."

Jeff frowned and started the engine. This was where he was getting off. As he backed out of the parking space, Billy Graham's words and a song Michelle had once sung began playing tag in his mind.

"Running from who, running from
where—
On my way to where am I going . . ."

On and on he drove. He had to get away. Mechanically he steered the van, and it seemed to stop automatically at the signs and signal lights.

The van coughed to a stop. Out of gas! Jeff maneuvered the van to the side of the road as best he could and pulled a red can out of the back. He walked and walked.

"On my way to where have I been?
On my way to what am I doing?
Something 'round me
I don't know
Coming on strong and
following where I go."

Deep in thought, he walked back to the van and poured the contents of the can into the gas tank. Across the road a car stopped, and a girl got out on the passenger's side. She shifted her backpack over her shoulder and looked around uncertainly. When she spied Jeff, she crossed the road toward him.

"Telling me to try and look His way
But I don't know, I don't know.
Catch me, catch me if you can. . . ."

Jeff and the girl entered the truck stop restaurant. Between forksful which they hungrily stuffed into their mouths, they talked animatedly and attempted to become acquainted. The waitress set a coke and a beer in front of them.

"Help me slow down and find
   out who I am
Help me to pick up the pieces
Try to make the puzzle fit . . .
Catch me if you can . . ."

Jeff pulled the van into the motel driveway. While he went into the office, the girl stayed in the car.

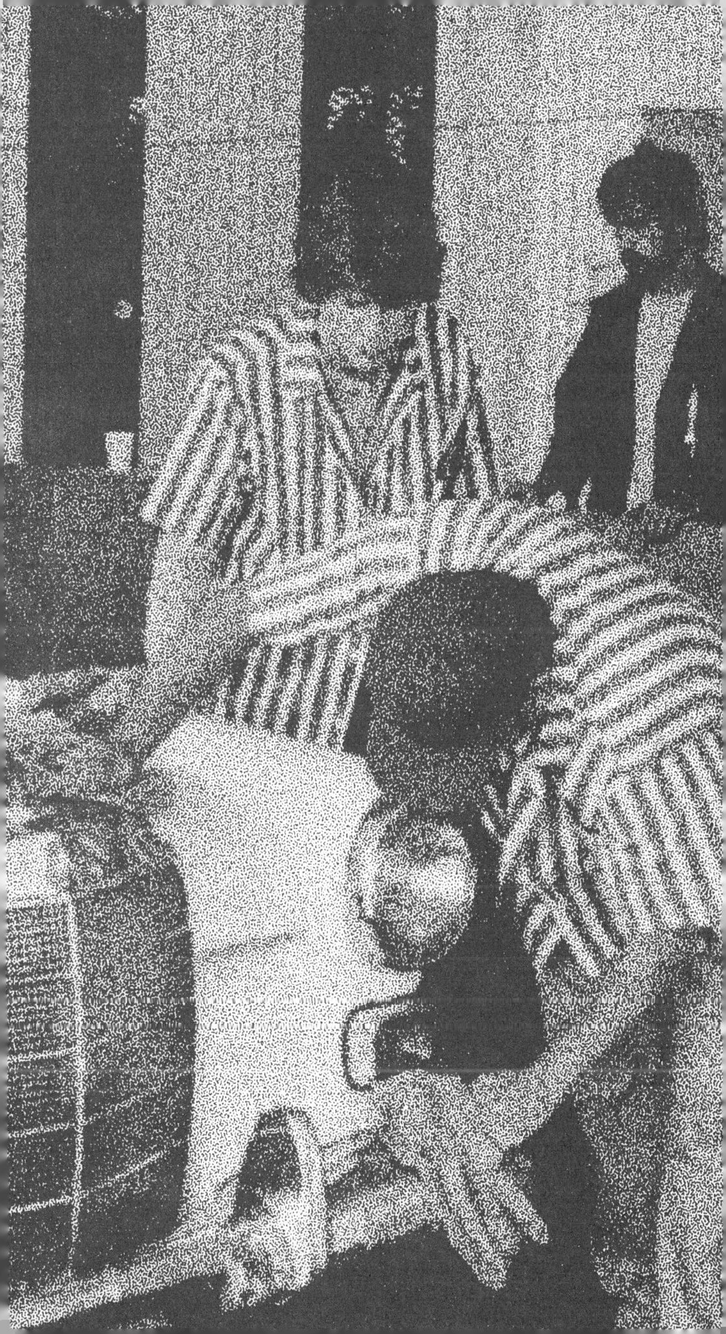

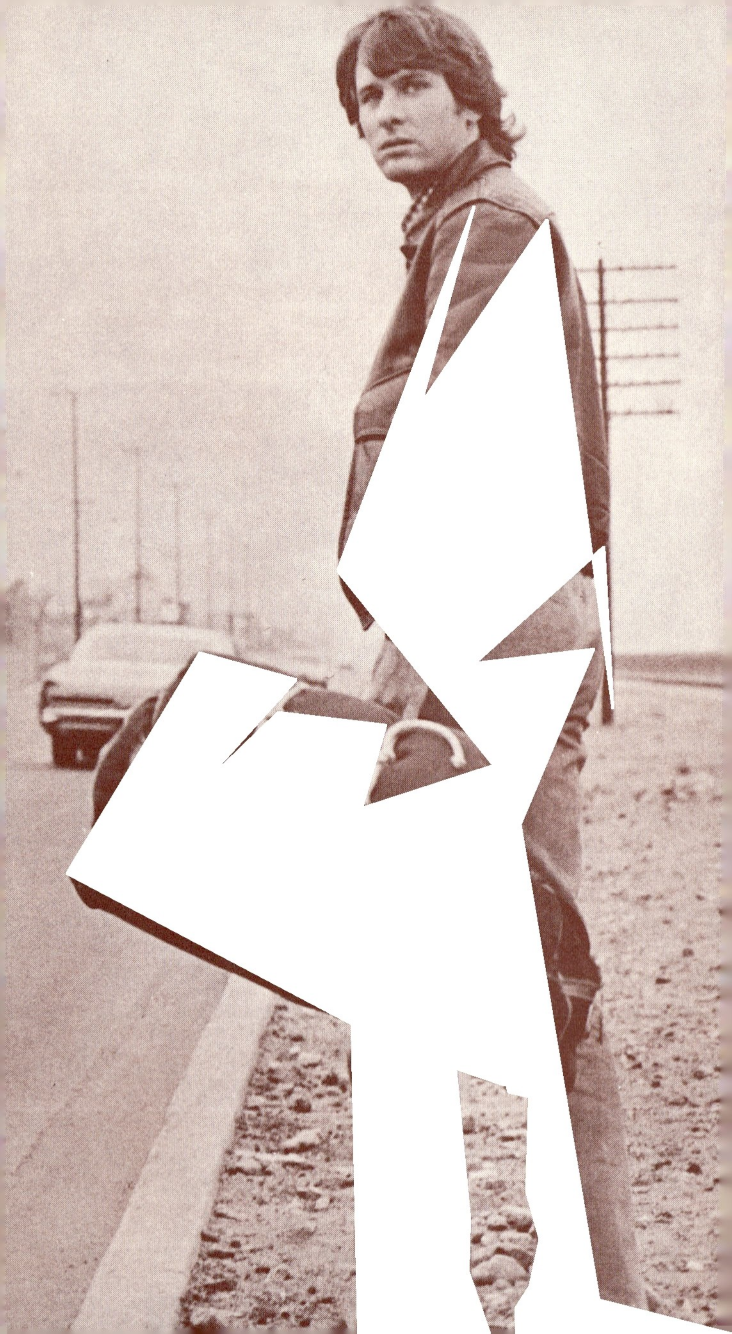

CHAPTER 10

As the sunlight began to force its way into the room, Jeff awoke with a start. He was alone. As the emptiness and loneliness hit him once again, he put his head in his hands.

"Catch me!
 Running away to where's all
  the sunshine . . .
 On my way to goodbye rain . . ."

The sign above the lot proclaimed "Sierra Auto Sales, Inc." Jeff pulled out his sleeping bag and other gear, and before he left his van, he again counted the cash he had been given for it. As he headed toward the road, the wind began to blow gustily.

"On my way to open some door
 On my way to what and where
  and more."

That night he slept in a deserted old building. Someone had evidently given up any plans for remodeling it, and pieces of lumber and shingles were strewn about outside and inside on the floor. He rolled up his sleeping bag and headed for the open highway.

> "Coming on strong and following
>   where I go
>   Telling me to try and look
>   His way."

Money for the next week's lodging was earned at a carwash. Dressed in his red-and-white striped attendant's shirt, Jeff wiped the car's dashboard as the water from the carwash sprayed the windshield.

> "To find the things I lost from
>   yesterday."

As the car finished its journey through the washers, Jeff jumped out and joined the other attendants in wiping it off. He bent down to dry off the rear fender. His eyes zeroed in on a blue and white bumper sticker which read, "Give Jesus a Chance."

> "Catch me, catch me if you can . . ."

Jeff walked on down the road. The highway was hot and dusty.

> "Help me slow down and find out
>   who I am."

His boots were broken down, and he staggered, barely able to keep walking as the cars whizzed by.

"Help me pick up the pieces,
    try to make the puzzle fit . . ."

As Jeff stood with his thumb out, the cars continued to pass him by.

"Catch me, oh catch me
Catch me if you can."

After a few days of hitchhiking and bumming, a growth of stubble began to sprout on Jeff's face.

Finally, a green and white pickup stopped for him. He tossed his gear in the back and gratefully got in.

"Catch me!"

□

Wearily Jeff staggered up the stairs to Michelle's apartment. He slowly reached her door, hesitated, and then knocked.

The door opened, and there stood Michelle. Her expression changed to surprise, then almost to shock.

Sheepishly he looked at her. "Hi." He gave her a small, embarrassed smile. "Do you have any more of that—Christian love left for a guy with an empty tank?"

Speechless, Michelle stared at his travel-weary profile. For a reply, she stood back from the door, a silent invitation to enter.

☐

Jeff and Michelle strolled along the breakwater, their minds locked deep in conversation.

"It seems like, uh, such a cop-out to just give in to Him." Michelle didn't say anything, and she let Jeff continue talking. "He hasn't left anything for me to do."

Gently she declared. "You have to believe—that takes faith."

He glanced at her; then he looked back down at the ground. "Yeah, well—yeah! Well, if He's God, He knows I don't understand it all."

"If He's the 'Hound of Heaven,' He'll know when you've stopped running...," Michelle countered.

They stopped walking for a moment and faced each other. Then they walked on as Jeff continued to ponder.

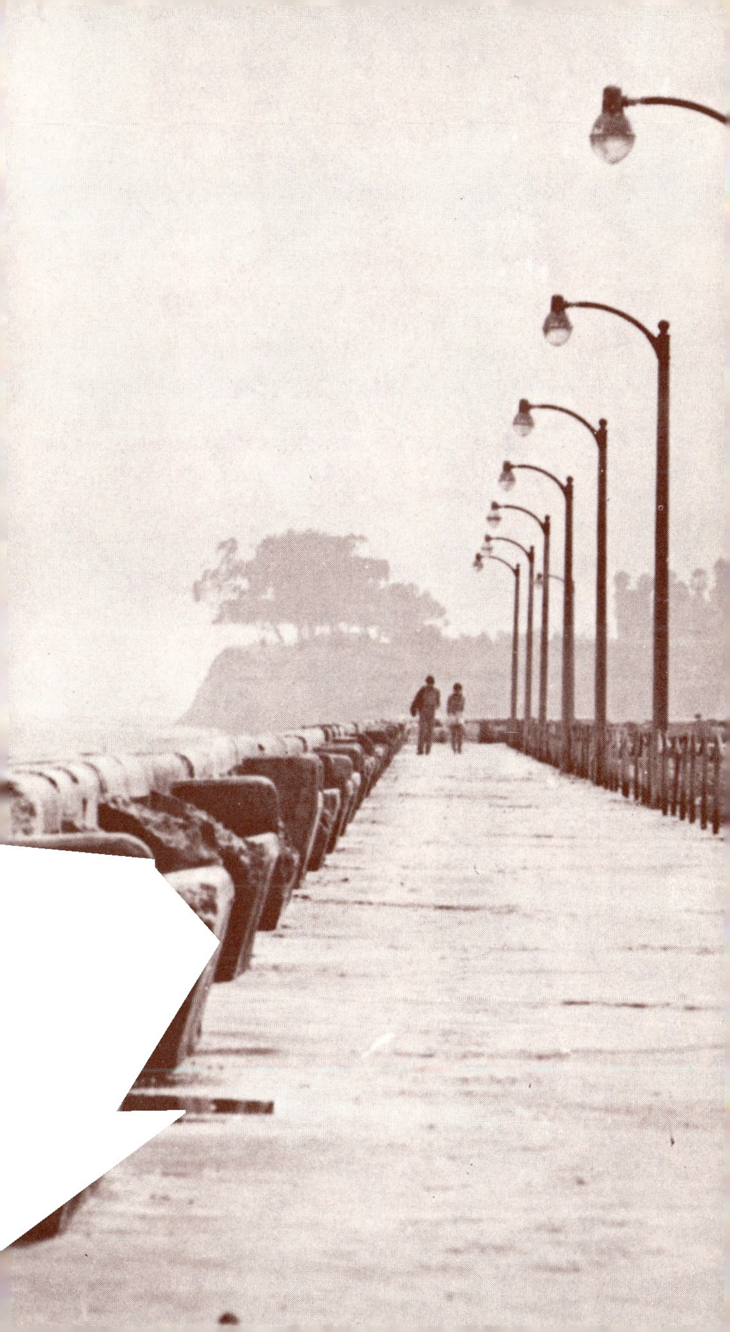

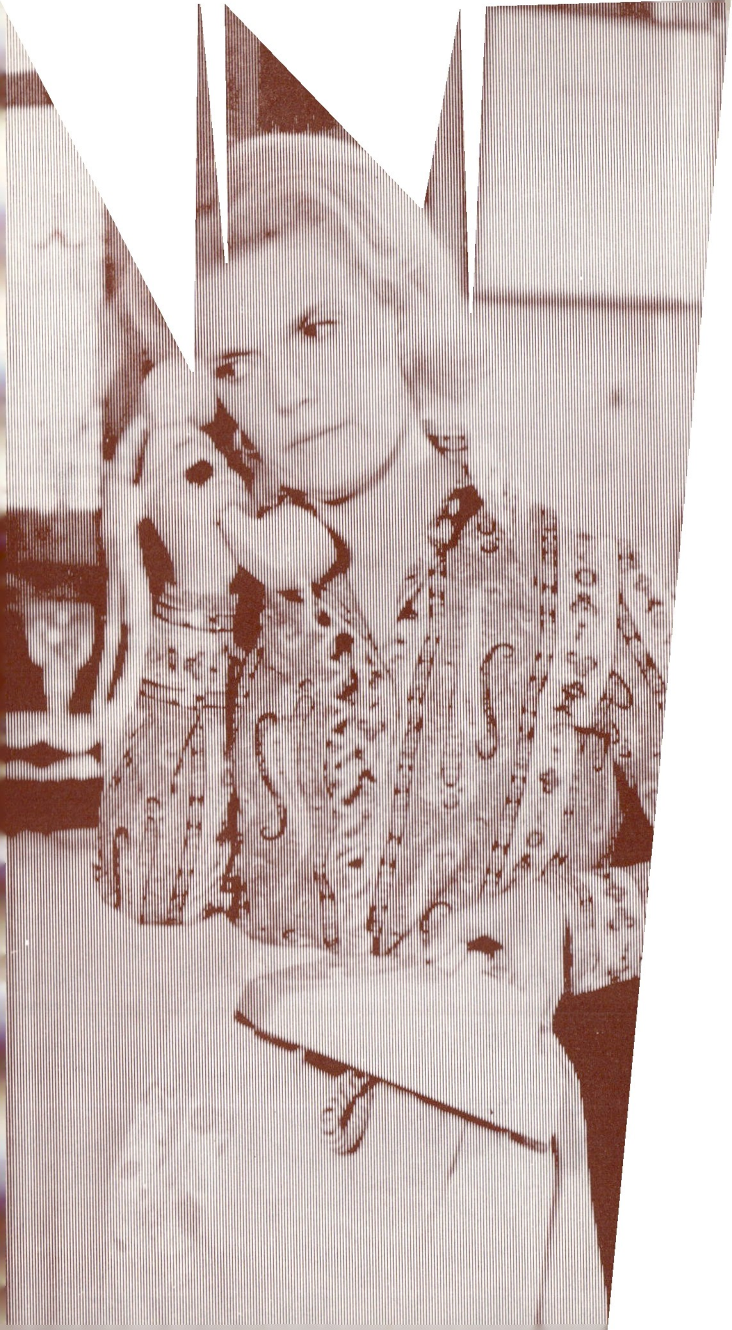

CHAPTER 11

Fran finished tucking the bedspread in around the pillow just as the phone began to ring.

"Hello? . . . Well, hi!" As she listened, her face lit up with hope and excitement. "Thanks!" She hung up and rushed downstairs. "Warren . . . Warren . . . Warren!"

He was on the patio cleaning his golf clubs as Fran rushed up to him.

"Michelle just called. She said we should come to the park."

"What for?" asked Warren.

"Well, she says that Jeff's there!"

☐

On top of the hill a couple of young people strummed guitars as the group sang together.

"Someone's praying, Lord
   Kum ba ya
Someone's praying, Lord
   Kum ba ya

Someone's praying, Lord
   Kum ba ya
Oh, Lord, Kum ba ya."

For a moment, there was some quiet chatter as they finished the song. Then a girl began to speak.

"I'd always been strong and independent until my family started breaking up for the second time. And I realized how weak I really was, how I needed somebody who's strong and whose love was constant. I had some friends who told me about Jesus Christ, and I really knew that I needed Him, and that He really wanted me."

Jeff seemed troubled as he listened, but Michelle's face wore a serene expression.

"I just couldn't help but respond to His unending love," the girl concluded.

There were murmurs of approval and a few "Praise the Lords" from the crowd, and another girl began to speak.

"He loves us no matter what. No matter what we've ever been or—anything. You know, it's not an 'I love you, but . . . ,' or an 'I love you, if . . . .' I love you. Period. And that's the love He gives us to love each other, and I just praise God for it."

Now both Jeff and Michelle were engrossed in the testimonies, and a blond boy stood up.

"Like I felt like I was lost, and you know, like twenty-five years. Like I used heroin for seven years. Like I've been in the penitentiary, like I felt like I never belonged all my life. Like I felt something was always missing inside of me. And now like I feel whole, I feel complete. And it's through Jesus Christ."

There were murmurs and some said "Amen" as he sat down. Several young people were now eager to share.

"You know, I just really praise God for the way He's forgiven me all the wrong that I've done, for writing people off, and for hurting people. But I know that I've been forgiven, not only by the people that I've offended. When I've gone back to ask their forgiveness, they've forgiven me. But especially Jesus Christ—He's forgiven me, and He's the one that I really wrote off."

A dark-haired boy in a flowered shirt began to speak. "In coming out of the drug culture, I found one of the biggest hangups for me was that I was never willing to admit that I was wrong or that I could possibly be sinful or something. And I found that when I accepted Christ at the age of eighteen—all I had to do was just be myself, and that's the kind of relationship I found that God wanted with me."

Jeff leaned his chin on his knee as he listened and reflected on what was being said.

A girl started to talk. "There was a girl in my class who, uh, started talking about Christ, and I couldn't believe it, because she really seemed to be, uh, a semi-intellectual person, and I couldn't bring the two together. And one by one all my intellectual arguments started breaking down, and Christ is in my life.

"And, you know, it's not hard to be alone now.... It's not hard to be alone at night. Because I know that God is really there."

Jeff took a deep breath.

"After awhile I just stopped running, I guess." The girl finished speaking.

Jeff turned to Michelle. "Well, I guess the chase is over." He stood up and sighed deeply before he began talking. "I've been doing a lot of searching, but I've—I've decided to trust Jesus. I—I need for Him to give me—well, for one thing, love. I don't really know what's going to happen from here on. But I do know that I need Jesus. And I—I figure He—He can show me the way."

Several young people murmured,

"Praise the Lord," and the guitarists began playing and singing.

> "What shall I give unto the Lord
> For all, for all, for all He's
> done for me—
> I'll take the gift of salvation
> And call, and call, and call upon
> the name of the Lord."

As Michelle looked at Jeff, her face reflected wonder and joy. He kissed her on the head and held her tightly for a few moments. As the song continued, Jeff shifted positions and sat down. Michelle looked out toward the path. Fran and Warren were approaching the group. Michelle turned and watched Jeff. He was struggling with his emotions. Now was his opportunity to practice his new-found faith in Jesus.

Suddenly he stood up and walked toward his parents. His parents stopped walking, and they looked at each other and at Jeff. He gestured helplessly. "I'm sorry."

Warren shook his hand. "That makes two of us, son."

They embraced, and Jeff continued, "I love you, Dad." He reached out to his mother, and she rushed into his arms.

"What shall I give unto the Lord?
>   I love you, I love you, I love you,
>   I love you, I love you, I love you
For all He's done for me?
>   I love you, I love you, I love you,
>   I love you, I love you, I love you
I'll take the gift of salvation
>   I love you, I love you, I love you,
>   I love you, I love you, I love you
And call upon the name of the Lord."

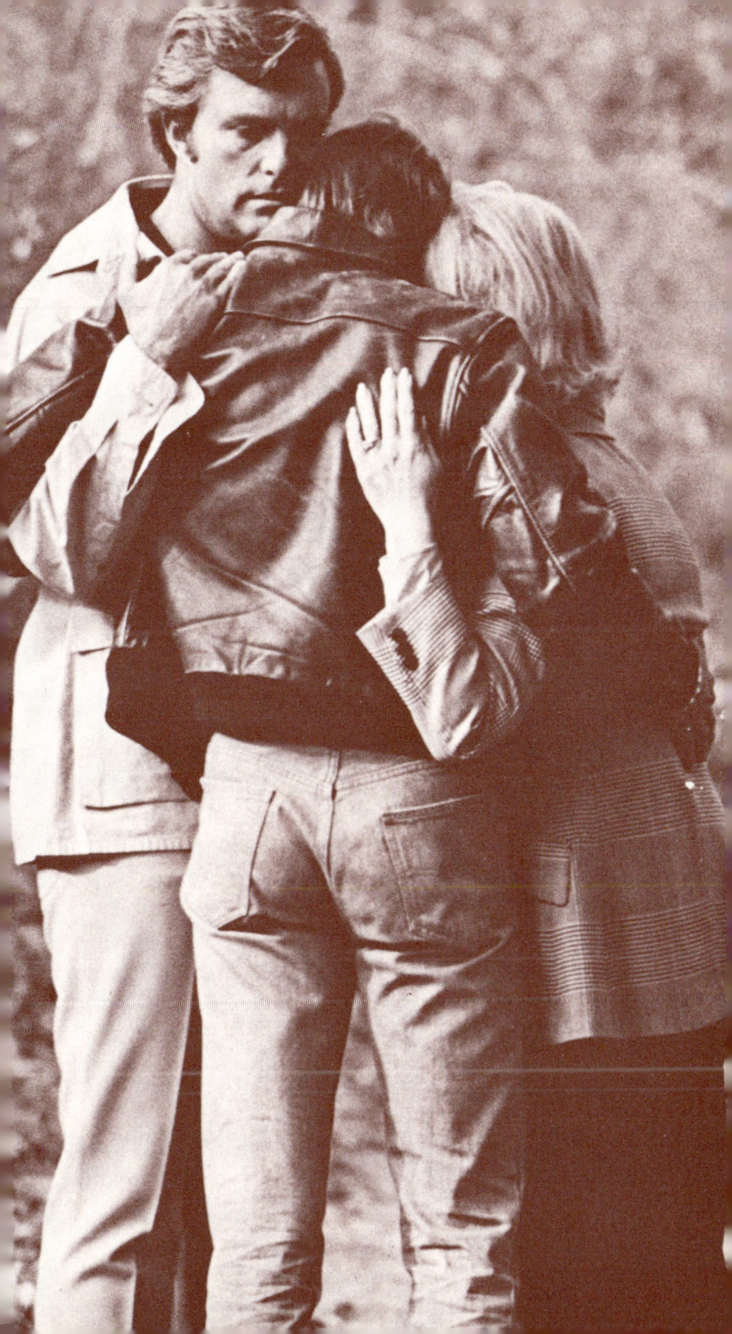

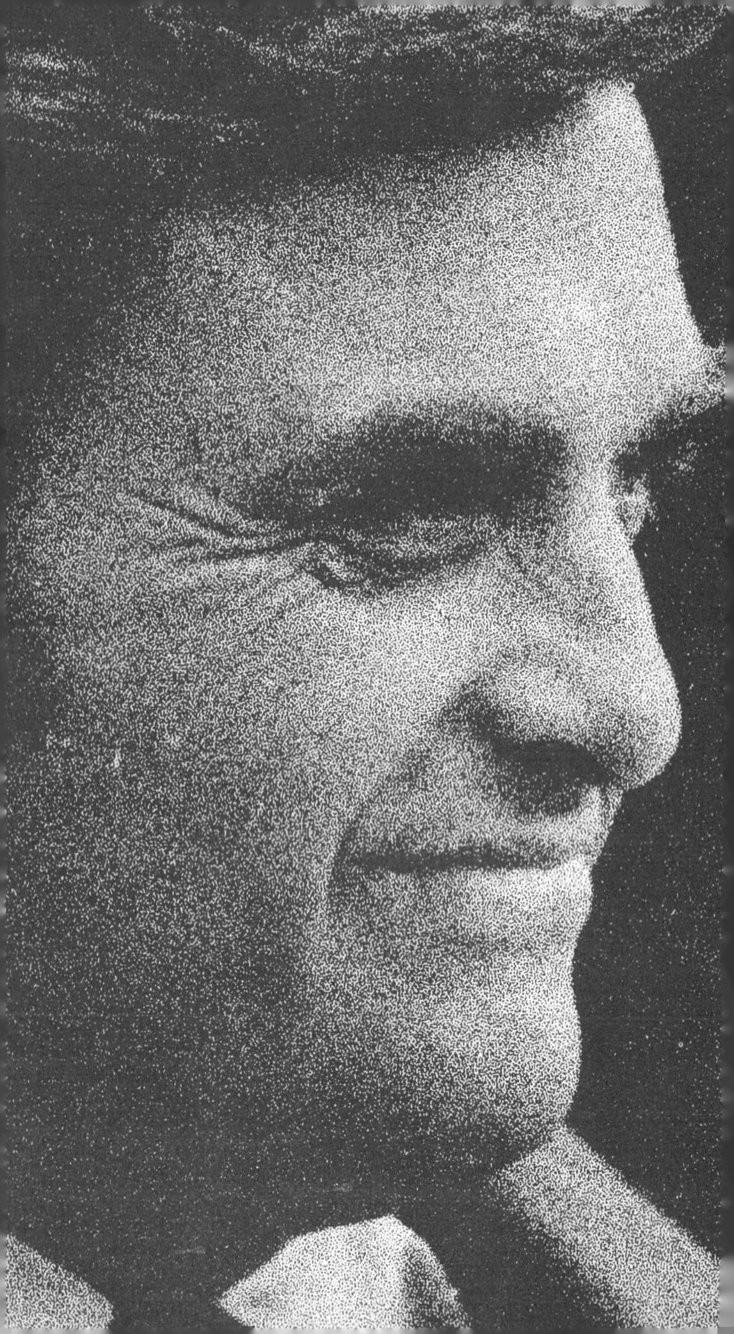

LETTERS from those who saw "TIME TO RUN"

Dear Dr. Graham:

Tonight I went and saw "Time To Run" at the Alex Theater in Glendale. I want to praise you for such a fantastic film! I'm a Catholic, middle-class, age 17. I have a car, a phone, and a job in addition to school!! But now I'm starting to realize, after seeing the film, that my car is a substitute for Jesus Christ! Like instant breakfast instead of a bacon-and-egg breakfast. They both satisfy your needs, but not your inner desires. I opened my door to Christ tonight with *new* hope because I have opened the door before and then slammed it in his face. And it has hurt me *more* than it has hurt him. So, I thought I should write to you (and I'm not much of a letter writing fan, either) to praise you on this film, and also to let you know that after I left the theater, I felt like a new person with a feeling of love, confidence, and inner warmth. It was beautiful!

                         R. D.
                         Hollywood, Calif.

Dear Sirs,

I really enjoyed your movie "Time To Run"! I go to the Lutheran church. I go to sixth grade Sunday school and church. My whole life is not all dedicated to Jesus Christ! I don't understand alot of things! I have friends who don't even know who Jesus Christ is. I would like to have some information on what I could do for myself and my friends. I really felt I needed someone to talk to after the movie. I realized that I really didn't know Jesus Christ as my personal Savior. Please will you help me know God better!!

R. F.
Colman, S.D.

Dear People,

I want to thank you for filming "A Time To Run." It states clearly the problems of today. But what's more, it gives an answer.

This film has helped me back to God. I am truly grateful for the opportunity. I hope and pray that others are as open and receptive to the message.

With God's love, peace, and understanding from the bottom of my heart.

P. G.
Millville, N.J.

Dear Gentlemen,

I wish to express my thanks for the picture, "Time To Run." It was one of the most wonderful films I have viewed. I am a fifteen-year-old Christian girl. It did something to me and something for our whole family. At the end of the movie there were a number who went forward to accept Jesus into their hearts.

D. B.
Penbrook. Penn.

Dear Sir,

Your movie was the most beautiful movie I've ever witnessed and one of the most moving experiences I've had.

I was involved in religion, but somehow ignorant of Christ. Now I am learning to live again through Christ.

I would like to share what I know with others and help them too.

                                      B. R.
                                    York, Penn.

Billy Graham,

I went to see "Time To Run" by recommendation of friends. I had accepted Christ about a year ago, but I seemed to be drifting away from God and his love. Then I went to "Time To Run" and something in my mind went *wow*! When they told us to come up front in the theater I went. We talked to a counselor and when I left that theater I knew God went with me.

J. G.
Glendale, Calif.

Dear Sir,

The best "investment" we ever made! Three of our four children went forward to accept Christ, along with two companions. (We took six, and five were saved!)

Thank you so much.

D. I.